THE MEN WHO KILLED ME

edited by **Anne-Marie de Brouwer**
& Sandra Ka Hon Chu
photographs by **Samer Muscati**

RWANDAN SURVIVORS

foreword by **Stephen Lewis**
afterword by **Eve Ensler**

THE MEN

OF SEXUAL VIOLENCE

WHO

KILLED

ME

Douglas & McIntyre

D&M PUBLISHERS INC.

Vancouver/Toronto/Berkeley

Douglas & McIntyre
A division of D&M Publishers Inc.
2323 Quebec Street, Suite 201
Vancouver BC Canada V5T 4S7
www.dmpibooks.com

Library and Archives Canada Cataloguing in Publication:
The men who killed me : Rwandan survivors of sexual violence / edited by
Sandra Chu and Anne-Marie de Brouwer.

ISBN 978-1-55365-310-3

1. Sexual abuse victims—Rwanda—Biography. 2. HIV-positive persons—
Rwanda—Biography. 3. Women—Violence against—Rwanda. 4. Women
and war—Rwanda. 5. Genocide—Rwanda. I. Chu, Sandra, 1977–
II. Brouwer, Anne-Marie de, 1975– III. Title.
HV6569.R95.M45 2009   967.57104'31   C2008-908075-0

Editing by Barbara Pulling
Copy editing by Eve Rickert
Cover and text design by Peter Cocking
Cover photograph of Marie Louise Niyobuhungiro by Samer Muscati
Printed and bound in Canada by Friesens
Printed on acid-free paper
Distributed in the U.S. by Publishers Group West

We gratefully acknowledge the financial support of the Canada Council
for the Arts, the British Columbia Arts Council, the Province of British
Columbia through the Book Publishing Tax Credit and the Government
of Canada through the Book Publishing Industry Development Program
(BPIDP) for our publishing activities.

To those who continue to suffer
from sexual violence in war

"History will judge us harshly if, once aware
of the nature and scope of this violence,
once outraged by its injustice, we do not
choose to act against it."

JAN EGELAND

*Former UN Under-Secretary-General for Humanitarian Affairs
and Emergency Relief Coordinator*

CONTENTS

FOREWORD

ON TWO OR THREE occasions, the notes in this remarkable volume refer to the report of a panel, appointed by the Organization for African Unity, that investigated the genocide in Rwanda between 1998 and 2000. The report was called *Rwanda: The Preventable Genocide*, and I was a member of the panel. The authors of *The Men Who Killed Me* will be familiar with the report, but most readers will not, so I'd like to relate a central anecdote.

Towards the end of our study, the seven-member panel convened in Kigali at the headquarters of the Polyclinique d'Espoir (the Polyclinic of Hope), a centre where women, assaulted and raped during the genocide, could gather seeking solace and friendship. The head of the Polyclinic read a statement conveying the anger and despair of the women over the dreadful sexual violence to which they'd been subjected, and then she asked the panel whether any of us would be willing to meet with three of the women, who desperately wanted to speak to us privately. Three members of the panel agreed, and we were taken to a tiny adjacent room, unbearably, stiflingly hot, furnished with three steel cots. The sun beat down mercilessly on the tin roof.

On one cot sat a woman who appeared to be about twenty. She had been raped repeatedly by the *génocidaires*. She had had blunt instruments and knives thrust into her vagina, was afflicted with fistula, and was HIV positive. She saw no reason for living. Sadly, so sadly, she died of AIDS two years later.

The second woman, in her thirties, was feisty and pugnacious and angry. "You're always asking us to forgive and forget," she said. "Well, why should I? None of the men who raped me have ever shown the slightest sign of remorse . . . why, then, should I forgive? In fact, when I look out my window in the morning, I see the men who raped me freely walking on their way to work. I will never forgive and forget."

The third woman, probably in her late forties, was a woman of immense dignity. She had been chained to a bed for three months and raped continuously by a dozen of her captors. She looked at us calmly and uttered words that are seared into my mind: "Whether I'm in the fields, or at home, or at market, I will never get the smell of semen out of my nostrils."

I remember standing in that unbearably baking room and thinking to myself, "Has the world gone mad? How are these things possible at the end of the twentieth century?"

Many of the testimonies in this book are even more disturbing and horrific. They give witness to the virulent misogyny that poisons and debases so much of the contemporary world.

Alas, Rwanda was but the precursor. There is a contagion of sexual violence sweeping parts of Africa: Liberia, Kenya, Zimbabwe, the Democratic Republic of Congo. Taken altogether, it can be seen as a war on women. And what is most disturbing is that the whole world knows, especially the UN Security Council and the countries that are the world's great powers, and virtually nothing is done about it.

I will admit that I don't understand. I am utterly bewildered; it's inexplicable to me. I don't understand what possesses men to behave with such bestiality, and I just cannot fathom why the world does nothing. The only possible explanation is that gender inequality—appropriately called femicide in this context—is fiercely rooted in the human psyche.

I don't know how we'll bring it to an end. But of course I know we must. And the stories in this book, however painful, are exactly what is needed to jolt the world into sanity.

STEPHEN LEWIS
December 8, 2008

INTRODUCTION

L IKE ALL BOOKS, this one began with an idea. As colleagues at a women's rights organization in The Hague, Anne-Marie and Sandra worked closely on a variety of issues related to sexual violence in war. Rwanda became a frequent topic of conversation as our friendship grew. The war-ravaged nation, known as the "country of a thousand hills," had, in effect, become Anne-Marie's second home; not only had she visited and worked in Rwanda over the years, but she had developed a deep friendship with a young Rwandan woman who had survived traumatic sexual violence during the genocide. We discussed the possibility of creating a venue for this woman and others like her to bring forth their experiences. Between 250,000 and 500,000 women and girls were raped in this tiny country between April and July 1994. Despite numerous accounts of the genocide, including coverage about perpetrators standing trial before the International Criminal Tribunal for Rwanda, the voices of rape survivors were notably absent.

In 2007, a few days before Christmas, we visited Solace Ministries, a survivor-run grassroots organization in Kigali that works with widows and orphans of the genocide, offering food, housing, HIV medication, counselling, income-generating projects and spiritual care. We were amazed by both the strength of the women we talked to and the invaluable support they provided for each other as survivors with a common bond. We decided then we would do whatever we could to share their stories. Our friend Samer, who was in Rwanda doing development work, suggested that photographs could bring another dimension to survivors' accounts of their experiences.

After months of working on the book abroad—Anne-Marie in The Hague and Sandra and Samer in Toronto—we returned to Rwanda in the summer of 2008 to complete the testimonials. We interviewed each survivor on three or four occasions. This approach worked well, since it lessened the trauma for survivors and gave us time to review the testimonials and ask follow-up questions. At each stage of the process, we obtained consent from the survivors, assuring them they could end the interview or withdraw from the book at any time. During the last session with each person, we read the entire testimonial aloud for their approval. All but one survivor we interviewed decided to continue with the project, but three requested that their faces not be recognizable in their photographs.

Throughout the interviews, the awe-inspiring staff of Solace Ministries were on hand to assist with translation and, if necessary, with counselling. With them we attended a *gacaca*, a traditional court that adjudicates crimes committed during the Rwandan genocide, to support a colleague in testifying against a former neighbour who had murdered her husband.

One afternoon towards the end of the process, we were packing up to leave the interview room when a tall, elegant woman approached us. She pleaded for us to listen to her story. She wanted the world to know the terrible things that had been done to her, she said. With a steady voice and a distant gaze, she told us about the unimaginable violence she had witnessed and experienced, then shared her fears for the future of her children. At that moment, we realized the book was already having a positive impact. These survivors felt that others cared enough to listen.

Once the interviews were complete, Samer travelled across Rwanda photographing survivors in their homes and areas where they experienced the genocide. What he saw shocked him. Most survivors live in rundown shacks with no electricity or running water. Some still live within walking distance of those who committed violence against them. Many lost their entire families in the genocide and so live a great distance from any support. In addition, a horrifying 70 per cent of survivors of sexual violence in Rwanda are now HIV positive. They are often stigmatized because of their condition, and the disease makes it difficult for many people to earn an income.

By sharing their testimonials, these survivors—sixteen women and one man—strive to keep the memory of the genocide alive. They urge the international community to refuse to permit such atrocities to happen again. The violence they suffered battered their bodies and extinguished their dreams. Incredibly, however, these survivors stand defiant. In the face of all odds, they have opted to bring to light the crimes that rape survivors have historically endured in silence. We feel privileged to have witnessed their immense courage, their hope and their will to continue. They have taught us how important it is to remember our common humanity.

The authors' proceeds from the sales of *The Men Who Killed Me* will be donated to Mukomeze (Kinyarwanda for "empower her"), a sponsorship program for girls and women raped during the genocide in Rwanda. In this way, we hope to help not only the survivors interviewed here but the thousands of others who were not. The women and young man featured in this book have profoundly changed our lives. We hope that their stories will do the same for you.

ANNE-MARIE DE BROUWER
SANDRA KA HON CHU
SAMER MUSCATI

RWANDA

★ National capital
◉ Prefecture capital
● Town, village

DEMOCRATIC
REPUBLIC OF
CONGO

Butaro
Kidaho
Ruhengeri
Kirambo
Busogo
NORTHERN
PROVINCE
Kora
Mutura
Nemba
Kagali
Goma
Gisenyi
Rushashi
Nyundo
Kabaya
Ngaru
WESTERN
Kiyumba
Ngororero
Bulinga
PROVINCE
Runda
Mabanza
Gitarama
Kibuye
Birambo
SOUTHERN
Gishyita
Bwakira
PROVINCE
Rwamatamu
Masango
Ruhango
Kaduha
Gatagara
Rwe002
Nyanza
Kamembe
Gisakura
Karaba
Rusatira
Bukavu
Cyangugu
Rwumba
Gikongoro
Karama
Cyimbogo
Kitabi
Nyakabuye
Bugumya
Karengera
Butare
Ruramba
Gisagara
Bugarama
Munini
Busoro
Runyombyi

Nyabarongo

River

Akanyaru River

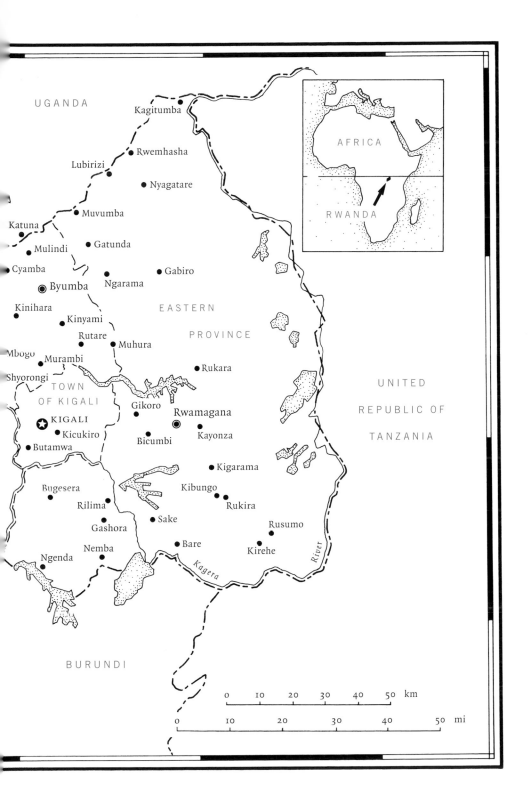

UGANDA

Kagitumba

Rwemhasha

Lubirizi

Nyagatare

Muvumba

Katuna

Gatunda

Mulindi

Cyamba

Gabiro

Byumba

Ngarama

EASTERN

Kinihara

Kinyami

PROVINCE

Rutare

Muhura

Mbogo

Murambi

Rukara

Shyorongi

TOWN

OF KIGALI

Gikoro

Rwamagana

KIGALI

Kicukiro

Bicumbi

Kayonza

Butamwa

Kigarama

Bugesera

Kibungo

Rilima

Rukira

Sake

Rusumo

Gashora

Bare

Kirehe

Nemba

Ngenda

Kagera

River

BURUNDI

UNITED

REPUBLIC OF

TANZANIA

AFRICA

RWANDA

| 0 | 10 | 20 | 30 | 40 | 50 | km |

| 0 | 10 | 20 | 30 | 40 | 50 | mi |

1

THE ROOTS
OF SEXUAL
VIOLENCE
IN RWANDA

"It has probably become more
dangerous to be a woman than a
soldier in an armed conflict."

PATRICK CAMMAERT

former division commander of the
United Nations Organization Mission
in the Democratic Republic of Congo

IN THE ONE HUNDRED DAYS of genocide that ravaged the small Central African nation of Rwanda from April until July 1994, about one million Tutsi and Hutu people were killed,[1] and an estimated 250,000 to 500,000 women and girls were raped.[2] According to a United Nations report, rape was the rule, its absence the exception.[3] Sexual violence occurred everywhere, and no one was spared. Grandmothers were raped in front of their grandchildren; girls witnessed their families being massacred before being taken as sex slaves; fathers were forced to have sex with their daughters. Many women were murdered following rape. Almost all of the women who did survive the genocide were victims of sexual violence or were profoundly affected by it.[4]

Fifteen years later, the impact of the sexual violence endured by survivors continues to be monumental, threatening their daily survival. An astounding 70 per cent are HIV positive.[5] Recognizing this, the UN General Assembly passed a resolution in 2004 affirming that survivors of sexual violence are among those who face the greatest hardship in post-conflict Rwanda.[6] Gender inequality and gender-based violence existed in Rwanda prior to the genocide,[7] but the events of 1994 provided a backdrop for rape to be perpetrated against Tutsi women and their sympathizers on a mass scale. The ideology of Hutu power was underscored through the dehumanization of Tutsi women.

THE GENOCIDE IN Rwanda was one of the most ruthless and effective of all time. Ostensibly sparked by the death of Hutu President Juvénal Habyarimana, whose plane was shot down by unknown assailants above Kigali airport on April 6, 1994, the event was preceded by a complicated and bloody history between Tutsi and Hutu.

When Belgian colonialists arrived in Rwanda in 1916, they favoured the Tutsi minority over the Hutu majority. The Belgians viewed the Tutsi as more similar to Europeans and, therefore, deemed them to be more intelligent. The clergy in Rwanda were complicit in creating and maintaining divisions between Tutsi and Hutu.[8] Tutsi were awarded better jobs and had greater educational opportunities, a distinction reinforced by the development of separate educational systems. The Belgians classified them by their physical traits, too: they considered Tutsi to be tall, thin and light skinned and Hutu to be short, stout and darker skinned. In the early 1930s, to solidify the division between Tutsi and Hutu, the Belgians produced identity cards classifying individuals according to their ethnic group: Hutu, Tutsi or Twa.[9] These identity cards, still in use in the 1990s, led many Tutsi to their death by readily identifying them to the *génocidaires*.

The ethnic classification between Tutsi and Hutu was imposed despite their many commonalities. The two groups speak the same language, Kinyarwanda. They share a similar culture, and intermarriage was common between Tutsi and Hutu. The distinction between Tutsi and Hutu is more accurately defined as one of fluid socio-economic class than of ethnicity. Traditionally, Hutu were farmers and Tutsi were wealthier cattle herders. Hutu who accumulated wealth were often reclassified as Tutsi, and Tutsi bereft of property could be reclassified as Hutu.[10]

Resentment among the Hutu about the special treatment of Tutsi festered over the years. It culminated in a series of killings of Tutsi, beginning in 1959 with the unexpected death of the ruling Tutsi king, and continuing through Rwandan independence from Belguim in 1962, after a popular uprising drove out the Tutsi elite and installed a Hutu-dominated government. Between 1959 and 1973, more than 700,000 Rwandan Tutsi were exiled to neighbouring countries.[11] Tutsi refugees were barred from returning, despite many peaceful efforts to do so. Some joined the Rwandan Patriotic Front—the RPF, commonly referred to as the Inkotanyi—a political and military movement formed by Tutsi refugees in Uganda to

Family photos of children who perished during the violence
of 1994 on display at Kigali's Gisozi Genocide Memorial

demand Rwandan unity. On October 1, 1990, the RPF, seeking to pressure the ruling Rwandan government into a power-sharing agreement, invaded Rwanda from Uganda. They were repelled by troops from France and Zaire sent to reinforce the Rwandan government.[12] Tutsi living in Rwanda were blamed for the RPF attack, and the Rwandan government massacred about two thousand of them across the country in apparent retaliation.[13]

When President Habyarimana's plane was shot down on April 6, 1994, he was returning to Rwanda from peace negotiations with the RPF in Tanzania. The president was killed instantly, and with him, all hope for peace. Habyarimana's death served as a pretext for Hutu extremists to launch their one hundred days of genocide. Previously prepared execution lists were circulated showing the names of Tutsi and moderate Hutu (Hutu who were opposed to the oppression of Tutsi). The most influential, educated and wealthy among these people were the first to be killed. Even influential Hutu were not spared if they posed a threat to the extremists. Most notably, moderate Hutu Prime Minister Agathe Uwilingiyimana was assassinated at the Kigali UN compound on April 7, 1994.

Eradicating the Tutsi became the calling of Hutu extremists. They taunted their victims with threats to "return" them to Ethiopia, where the Tutsi allegedly originated; because of their lighter skin and narrower noses and chins, Tutsi were accused of being "of European stock." Within hours of Habyarimana's death, Hutu began killing and raping Tutsi, with the aim of complete annihilation. With the prospects for peace extinguished, the RPF invaded Rwanda. After ensuring that nationals of Western governments had safe passage out of the country, the world stood by silently and watched one of the worst massacres in human history.[14] The genocide ended only when the RPF overthrew the Hutu regime in July 1994.

THE SEXUAL VIOLENCE in Rwanda during the genocide was extreme in its brutality and systematic in its orchestration. Victims were selected predominantly on the basis of their gender and their Tutsi ethnicity. Age did not play a role in who was attacked: Tutsi women and girls of all ages were raped. The targeting of Tutsi girls and women was spurred in part by anti-Tutsi propaganda preceding the 1994 genocide, which alleged that the minority Tutsi population was a threat to the Hutu community. Radio and newspapers, to which most Rwandans had access, both played a major role in the genocide. To desensitize the Hutu masses, hate radio station Radio Télévision Libre des Mille Collines (RTLM) continuously referred to Tutsi as cockroaches and snakes.[15]

In the December 1990 issue of *Kangura*, an influential Rwandan newspaper, the sexuality of Tutsi women was one focus of the Hutu "Ten Commandments." In four of the "commandments," Tutsi women were portrayed as tools of the Tutsi community and as sexual weapons who would be used to weaken and ultimately destroy Hutu men.[16] Newspapers also featured cartoons that portrayed Tutsi women, including the moderate Hutu Prime Minister Agathe Uwilingiyimana, as sexual objects.[17]

Perpetrators often referred in the midst of rape to the supposed beauty and arrogance of Tutsi women; hate propaganda alleged that Tutsi women looked down on Hutu men and thought they were "too good" for them. Rape thus served as a means to degrade and subjugate Tutsi women. Sexual violence was also directed at Hutu women considered moderates: women who were married to Tutsi men, protected Tutsi individuals or were politically affiliated with Tutsi. Though much less frequently, sexual violence was perpetrated against Hutu women and girls with no affiliation with the Tutsi population—crimes made possible by the prevailing chaos during the conflict. Men, primarily of Tutsi ethnicity, were also sexually assaulted, often by the mutilation of their genitals, which were sometimes displayed in public. In some cases, Tutsi men and boys were forced to rape Tutsi women or were forced by Hutu women to have sex with them.

Women and girls were subjected to the full range of sexual atrocity. This included rape, gang rape, sexual slavery, forced incest, forced marriage, and amputation or mutilation of victims' breasts, vaginas and buttocks, or of features considered to be Tutsi, such as small noses or long fingers.[18] Even pregnant women were not spared.

An expert panel has reported that some HIV-positive perpetrators intentionally tried to transmit the virus by raping Tutsi women.[19] In the eyes of the Hutu perpetrators, infecting a Tutsi woman with HIV served as an effective means to infect her future sexual partners and any children she bore as well as to eventually kill her and leave her dependents without her support.[20] Some women abducted to be the personal slaves, or "wives," of Hutu men were forced to remain with their rapists after the genocide, in some cases moving to neighbouring countries with their captors.

Barbed wire surrounding École Technique Officielle memorial site near Kigali

At the time of the genocide, Rwanda's twelve prefectures were sub-divided into communes, sectors and cells, with cells being the most decentralized territorial unit of local government. Sexual violence took place in every part of the country, though the majority of cases occurred in the southern part of Rwanda, probably because these regions were among the last to fall under the control of the invading RPF.[21] Rape did occur inside victims' or perpetrators' houses, but more often it was commit-ted in plain view of others, at sites such as schools, churches, roadblocks and government buildings. Many women were also raped in the bushes where they had hidden to avoid being discovered. Frequently, rape victims' corpses were left spread-eagled in public view, as a reminder of the bru-tality and power of the genocide's perpetrators. In addition to the sexual violence they endured, many women witnessed crimes such as torture and murder committed against their loved ones. Many of them lost their houses and property.

The perpetrators of sexual violence were mostly members of the Hutu militia, the Interahamwe. But rapes were also committed by Presidential Guards, military soldiers of the Rwandan Armed Forces (FAR), the Rwan-dan police and civilians, as well as by international soldiers—most notably the French, who were stationed in the southwest of the country under a UN mandate called Opération Turquoise to supposedly establish and maintain a "secure humanitarian area."[22] Many government officials and leaders of the militia and the military were complicit. They knew that rape was being committed, and there is evidence that leaders encouraged or ordered their men to rape Tutsi women or condoned the commission of sexual violence by not intervening.[23] Hutu women from all walks of life also perpetrated sexual violence by raping boys and men, by violating Tutsi women with objects and by facilitating or ordering their rape.[24]

Compared with conflicts in other places, the sexual violence in Rwanda is notorious because of the organized propaganda, which contributed sig-nificantly to fuelling sexual violence against Tutsi women, the very public nature of the rapes and the level of ruthlessness directed towards women.[25] Today, shockingly, despite the many documented horrors during the geno-cide, there is a growing denial of what happened during those one hundred days in Rwanda and a resurgence of genocidal ideology in Rwanda and other countries.[26]

RAPE AND OTHER FORMS of sexual violence during conflict have historically been viewed as a private matter, seen as collateral damage inconsequential to the larger considerations of wartime politics or justified as an inevitable consequence of war, a necessary bounty for fighting men. However, following the Rwandan genocide in 1994 and the wars in the former Yugoslavia (1991–2001), numerous accounts brought to the fore the pervasive degree of sexual violence committed against women and girls. The use of rape in war had finally captured the world's attention, and sexual violence was transformed in people's understanding from the private actions of individuals to a public and political tool of aggression.

But despite the brazen nature of the sexual violence committed in Rwanda and the former Yugoslavia, such crimes were by no means new. During almost every conflict in the world, sexual violence has been perpetrated against women in various ways, often with complete impunity. Although sexual violence during conflicts has been documented as both widespread and systematic, perpetrators of these crimes have rarely been held accountable for their actions. Even today, it is common to hear the assertion that women who were raped and survived are "lucky" they were not killed, and there is a broad perception that rape is somehow a lesser crime not worth investigating.

While men may also be targeted in this way during conflict, sexual violence primarily affects women. Traditional attitudes towards women's rights tacitly condone violence against women. A culture of pre-existing gender inequality that turns a blind eye to sexual violence in the family helps create an environment for targeted violence against women during armed conflict. Social norms crumble during conflict: tolerance to violence increases, and communities begin to accept violence as a legitimate way of expressing anger and resolving issues. The environment during armed conflict is devoid of the social safety mechanisms that normally inhibit extreme and exaggerated forms of gender-based violence. When societies collapse, some men perceive a licence to rape. Sexual attacks in such situations may be crimes of opportunism, made possible by the breakdown of the usual protection mechanisms. In cases where a conflict pits one group against another, sexual violence may target one particular group of women and girls.

IN THE CONSERVATIVE social and cultural climate of Rwanda, women find it extremely difficult to speak openly about sexual violence. The stigma and discrimination experienced by rape survivors are compounded if they are living with HIV. A significant number of persons living with HIV in Rwanda have no access to antiretroviral (ARV) treatment, so for many, HIV-positive status means certain death.[27] Although some women aware of their HIV status have begun to speak more openly about their experiences during the genocide, HIV-positive individuals still suffer severe discrimination. Women may refrain from seeking medical treatment following rape because they fear being ostracized in their communities, including, sometimes, by their own husbands. The stigma attached to being a survivor of genocidal rape and, in many cases, also HIV positive, has led in Rwanda to the denial of women's rights to property and inheritance as well as of their access to employment. Rendering women economically and socially vulnerable makes them susceptible to further violence.

Much has been written about the use of rape and sexual violence during the Rwandan genocide, but survivors themselves have been notably absent from the discussion. The survivors who tell their stories in this book hope to change that.

NOTES

1. This number is provided by the Rwandan government on its Web site, www.gov.rw. While it is difficult to estimate the actual number of people killed during the genocide, numbers cited in various reports vary from 500,000 to more than one million deaths.

2. See Organization of African Unity, *Rwanda: The Preventable Genocide* (Addis Ababa, Ethiopia: OAU, 2000), para. 16.20. A 2007 study estimated the number of women raped during the Rwandan genocide to be just over 350,000. Most of them were Tutsi. The study emphasized that this number was very likely an underestimate. See Catrien Bijleveld and Aafke Morssinkhof, "Counting the Countless: Rape Victimisation During the Rwandan Genocide," forthcoming.

3. See UN Commission on Human Rights, *Question of the Violation of Human Rights and Fundamental Freedoms in Any Part of the World, with Particular Reference to Colonial and Other Dependent Countries and Territories. Report on the Situation of Human Rights in Rwanda*, submitted by Mr. René Degni-Segui under paragraph 20 of resolution s-3/1 of May 25, 1994, E/CN.4/1996/68, 1996, para. 16, www.unhchr.ch/Huridocda/Huridoca.nsf/0/aee2ff8ad005e2f6802566f30040a95a?Opendocument (last acessed January 30, 2009).

4. See Organization of African Unity, *Rwanda: The Preventable Genocide*, para. 16.20.

5. See Survivors Fund (SURF), *Statistics on Rwanda*, (London, undated), www.survivors-fund.org.uk/resources/history/statistics.php (last accessed August 30, 2008).

6. See UN General Assembly, *Resolution 59/137 of 10 December 2004 on Assistance to Survivors of the 1994 Genocide in Rwanda, Particularly Orphans, Widows and Victims of Sexual Violence*, A/RES/59/137, 2004.

7. For example, see Human Rights Watch, *Overview of Human Rights Developments—Rwanda* (New York: HRW, 1991 and 1993), www.hrw.org/reports/1992/WR92/AFW-07.htm#P451_159300 and www.hrw.org/legacy/reports/1994/WR94/Africa-06.htm (last accessed August 29, 2008); Amnesty International, *Rwanda: "Marked for Death," Rape survivors Living with HIV/AIDS in Rwanda* (London: Amnesty International, 2004), p. 2, www.amnesty.org/en/library/info/AFR47/007/2004 (last accessed January 29, 2009; and Christopher C. Taylor, "A Gendered Genocide: Tutsi Women and Hutu Extremists in the 1994 Rwanda Genocide," POLAR 22 (1999): 42–54. For a discussion of the position of women in Rwanda pre-genocide more generally, see Tor Sellström and Lennart Wohlgemuth, *The International Response to Conflict and Genocide: Lessons from the Rwanda Experience* (Uppsala: Steering Committee of the Joint Evaluation of Emergency Assistance to Rwanda, 1996).

8. See Stephanie Nieuwoudt, "Rwanda: Church Role in Genocide under Scrutiny," *Institute for War and Peace Reporting*, December 1, 2006, www.iwpr.net/?p=acr&s=f&o=325838&apc_state=henpacr (last accessed August 30, 2008).

9. The Twa, who are also referred to as "pygmies," are considered to be the first inhabitants of Rwanda and make up less than 1 per cent of the total population (about ten million in 2008). The Tutsi account for about 14 per cent and the Hutu for about 85 per cent of the total population in Rwanda. See CIA, *The World Factbook: Rwanda*, 2008, www.cia.gov/library/publications/the-world-factbook/geos/rw.html (last accessed August 29, 2008).

10. See Mahmood Mamdani, *When Victims Become Killers: Colonialism, Nativism, and the Genocide in Rwanda* (Princeton: Princeton University Press, 2001), p. 70.

11. See Kigali Memorial Centre, *Path to a 'Final Solution,'* (Kigali, undated), www.kigalimemorialcentre.org/old/genocide/rwanda/political.html (last accessed August 27, 2008).

12. For example, see Linda Melvern, "France and genocide: the murky truth," *The Times*, August 8, 2008.

13. See Human Rights Watch, *Overview of Human Rights Developments—Rwanda*, 1993.

14. For a personal account of the indifference of the world at the height of the Rwandan genocide, see Romeo Dallaire, *Shake Hands with the Devil* (Toronto: Vintage Canada, 2004). See also Samantha Power, *"A Problem from Hell:" America and the Age of Genocide* (New York: Perennial, 2004).

15. For example, see Russell Smith, "The impact of hate media in Rwanda," BBC News Online, December 3, 2003, http://news.bbc.co.uk/2/hi/africa/3257748.stm (last accessed August 30, 2008); and Yaroslav Trofimov, "As horror recedes in time, Rwanda still restrains press," *Wall Street Journal*, April 30, 2004.

16. Four of the Ten Commandments dealt specifically with Tutsi women: (1) "Every Hutu should know that a Tutsi woman, wherever she is, works for the interest of her Tutsi ethnic group. As a result, we shall consider a traitor any Hutu who: marries a Tutsi woman; befriends a Tutsi woman; employs a Tutsi woman as a secretary or a concubine"; (2) "Every Hutu should know that our Hutu daughters are more suitable and conscientious in their role as woman, wife, and mother of the family. Are they not beautiful, good secretaries and more honest?"; (3) "Hutu women, be vigilant and try to bring

your husbands, brothers and sons back to reason"; and (4) "The Rwandese Armed Forces should be exclusively Hutu. The experience of the October [1990] war has taught us a lesson. No member of the military shall marry a Tutsi."

17. In the December 1993 issue of *Power*, a Hutu publication, Tutsi women were portrayed as seductresses and RPF allies who were having sex with the Belgian UN peacekeepers of UNAMIR, considered by the Hutu to be RPF supporters. Another cartoon featured Prime Minister Agathe Uwilingiyimana in various sexual poses with other politicians. During the genocide, the prime minister was shot by Hutu extremists, and her naked lower torso was exposed with a beer bottle protruding from her vagina. See Jean-Pierre Chrétien, *Rwanda: les médias du génocide* (Paris: Karthala, 2005), pp. 336 and 368.

18. See Human Rights Watch, *Shattered Lives: Sexual Violence during the Rwandan Genocide and its Aftermath* (New York, 1996).

19. See Organization of African Unity, *Rwanda: The Preventable Genocide*, para. 16.19.

20. See Françoise Nduwimana, *The Right to Survive: Sexual Violence, Women and HIV/AIDS* (Montreal: International Centre for Human Rights and Democratic Development, 2004), p. 18, www.dd-rd.ca/site/_PDF/publications/women/hivAIDS.pdf (last accessed January 30, 2009).

21. For example, the following areas were taken by the RPF on the following days in 1994: Mulindi and Nyagatare (April 8), Byumba (April 21), Rwamagana (April 27), Rusumo (April 29–30), Kigali airport and Kanombe military camp (May 22–23), Nyanza (May 29), Kabgayi (June 2), Gitarama (June 13), Butare (July 3), Kigali (July 4), Ruhengeri (July 14), Gisenyi (July 17). Taken from Phillip Green, "Map of RPF advance into Rwanda (April–July 1994)," in Linda Melvern, *A People Betrayed: The Role of the West in Rwanda's Genocide* (London: Zed Books, 2000), p. xii. See also National Service of Gacaca Jurisdictions, *Summary of Persons Prosecuted of Having Committed Genocide* (Kigali, undated), www.inkiko-gacaca.gov.rw/pdf/abaregwa%20english.pdf (last accessed October 27, 2008). This overview reveals that the majority of identified perpetrators are from the Southern Province (353,297, or 43.2 per cent of 818,564). On January 1, 2006, the twelve prefectures of Rwanda were abolished and replaced with five provinces. The Southern Province comprises the former prefectures of Gikongoro, Gitarama and Butare.

22. Evidence of French involvement in the raping of Tutsi women came to light in Republic of Rwanda, *Commission nationale indépendante chargée de rassembler les éléments de preuve montrant l'implication de l'Etat français dans la préparation et l'exécution du génocide perpétré au Rwanda en 1994, Rapport*, (Kigali, 2007). Opération Turquoise existed between June 23, 1994, and August 21, 1994.

23. A notorious example is Mayor Akayesu from Taba commune in Gitarama prefecture, who was sentenced at the International Criminal Tribunal for Rwanda to life imprisonment. Among his convictions were rape and sexual violence as genocide and crimes against humanity. See *The Prosecutor v. Jean-Paul Akayesu: Judgement of the Rwanda Tribunal*, Case No. ICTR-96-4-T, September 2, 1998.

24. See African Rights, *Rwanda—Not So Innocent· When Women Become Killers* (Kigali, 1995). Some 3,000 women accused of participating in the genocide were imprisoned in Rwanda in 2002. See Nicole Itano, "3,000 Rwandan Women Await Trials for Genocide," *Women's Enews*, December 20, 2002, www.womensenews.org/article.cfm?aid=1152 (last accessed August 30, 2008). One notable example of a woman who allegedly ordered Hutu men to rape Tutsi women is Pauline Nyiramasuhuko, the former Minister of Family and Women's Development, who at the time of writing is standing trial at the Rwanda Tribunal in Tanzania.

Nyiramasuhuko was the first woman to be indicted by an international criminal tribunal. In addition to other charges, she was charged with rape as genocide, a crime against humanity and a war crime.

25. See testimony of Binaifer Nowrojee, expert witness before the Rwanda Tribunal, in *The Prosecutor v. Théoneste Bagasora and others: Transcripts*, Case No. ICTR-98-41-T, July 12, 2004, p. 34.

26. For example, see "Rwanda 'still teaching genocide,'" BBC *News Online*, January 17, 2008, http://news.bbc. co.uk/2/hi/africa/7194827.stm (last accessed August 30, 2008), which reported that genocidal ideology is still being taught in a number of schools in Rwanda. In June 2008, Rwanda adopted a new law that criminalizes the spreading of "genocide ideology." The range of sentences for a conviction is harsh and includes life imprisonment. See Human Rights Watch, *Law and Reality: Progress in Judicial Reform in Rwanda* (New York, 2008); see also Leslie Evans, "The People Who Cover Up Genocide," UCLA *International Institute*, March 3, 2005, www.international.ucla.edu/article.asp?parentid=21398 (last accessed January 25, 2009).

27. According to the World Health Organization, an estimated 7,800 Rwandans died of AIDS in 2007, out of approximately 150,000 HIV-positive Rwandans. See UNAIDS/WHO, *Epidemiological Fact Sheets on HIV and AIDS, 2008 Update*, www.who.int/globalatlas/predefinedReports/EFS2008/full/EFS2008_RW.pdf (last accessed November 30, 2008). Rwanda has made some progress in increasing access to ARV treatment, with 44,395 Rwandans, or 53 per cent of adults, in need of ARV treatment now receiving it. This is a 50-fold increase from 2002, when there were only 870 people receiving ARV treatment. See Republic of Rwanda, UNGASS *Country Progress Report: Republic of Rwanda, Reporting Period: January 2006 to December 2007*, Draft (Kigali, 2008), p. 27.

SEXUAL VIOLENCE
DURING CONFLICT

THE MAGNITUDE OF sexual violence in conflict situations will never be fully known, since the stigma associated with being a victim discourages women and girls from reporting the crime. Many victims are also killed following rape. However, there are many reported instances, of which these are a few examples:

EUROPE: During World War I, 1914–18, rape, forced prostitution and other forms of sexual violence were directed towards women in Belgium and France, largely by the German army and the armies of other Axis powers. See Kelly D. Askin, *War Crimes against Women: Prosecution in International War Crimes Tribunals* (The Hague: Martinus Nijhoff Publishers, 1997), p. 42.

ASIA: Between 20,000 and 80,000 girls and women were raped in Nanjing, China, after the city fell to the Japanese Imperial Army in December 1937. See "Chinese City Remembers Japanese 'Rape of Nanjing,'" CNN, December 13, 1997. Sexual mutilation and murder following rape were common, and up to 200,000 women were also forced into military prostitution as "comfort women" in different countries in Asia. See Ustinia Dolgopol and Snehal Paranjape, *Comfort Women: An Unfinished Ordeal: Report of a Mission* (Geneva: International Commission of Jurists, 1994).

EUROPE: Rape and other forms of sexual violence, including forced prostitution and forced sterilization, were committed against women in Europe during World War II, 1939–45, on a large scale. German soldiers raped Russian women and girls, including Jewish women, and the Russian army raped German women and girls on a massive scale. See Kelly D. Askin, *War Crimes against Women*, pp. 52–61, 71–73, 88–91. Soviet Red Army soldiers are estimated to have raped two million German women and girls by the end of World War II. See Antony Beevor, "They Raped Every German Female from Eight to 80," *The Guardian*, May 1, 2002.

BANGLADESH: During the 1971 invasion of Bangladesh by Pakistan, at least 200,000 women were raped, thousands of whom later gave birth. See Gendercide Watch, *Case Study: Genocide in Bangladesh, 1971* (Edmonton, undated), www.gendercide.org/case_bangladesh.html (last accessed October 25, 2008).

CAMBODIA: Approximately 250,000 Cambodian women were forced into marriage during the Khmer Rouge regime's violent rule, 1975–79. See Amnesty International, *Making Violence Against Women Count: Facts and Figures—A Summary* (London, 2004).

PERU: During Peru's civil war, 1980–2000, more than 500 cases of sexual violence against women and girls were documented. The overwhelming majority of cases were not reported to the authorities. See Truth and Reconciliation Commission, *Final Report of the Truth and Reconciliation Commission of Peru (TRC)*, vol. 8, *The Factors that Made the Violence Possible* (2003).

HAITI: Between 1991 and 1994, the Commission Nationale de Vérité et Justice documented 140 cases of "political rape"—rape perpetrated against women because of their husbands' alleged political affiliation—but estimated that, in view of non-reporting and other circumstances, the actual incidence could be as much as twelve times higher. See Commission Nationale de Vérité et Justice, *Si M Pa Rele: 29 Septembre 1991–14 Octobre 1994* (Port-au-Prince: Ministère National de la Justice de la République d'Haiti, 1996), p. 84.

SIERRA LEONE: As many as 64,000 internally displaced women were subject to war-related sexual violence between 1991 and 2001. See Marie

Vlachova and Lea Biason, eds., *Women in an Insecure World* (Geneva: Geneva Centre for the Democratic Control of Armed Forces, 2005).

BOSNIA-HERZEGOVINA: During the 1992–95 Bosnian war, an estimated 20,000 to 50,000 women were raped, representing 1 to 2 per cent of the total pre-war female population. See UNICEF International Child Development Centre, *Women in transition, MONEE project, CEE / CIS / Baltics Regional Monitoring Report No. 6* (Florence, 1999), p. 85.

KOSOVO: During the war of 1998–99, thousands of Albanian women and girls living in Kosovo were victims of sexual violence. See Human Rights Watch, *Federal Republic of Yugoslavia—Kosovo: Rape as a Weapon of "Ethnic Cleansing"* (New York, 2000).

DEMOCRATIC REPUBLIC OF CONGO (DRC): Tens of thousands of women and girls were raped or otherwise subjected to sexual violence during the conflict in the DRC between 1998 and 2003. See Human Rights Watch, *Seeking Justice: The Prosecution of Sexual Violence in the Congo War* (New York, 2005). Between 2005 and 2007, more than 32,000 cases of rape and sexual violence were registered in the province of South Kivu, DRC, alone. See John Holmes, "Congo's Rape War," *Los Angeles Times*, October 11, 2007, www.latimes.com/news/opinion/la-oe-holmes11oct11,0,6685881.story?coll=la-opinion-center (last accessed November 30, 2008).

EAST TIMOR: The Indonesian military and local militias committed hundreds of documented cases of sexual violence against girls and women during the 1999 siege. See Galuh Wandita, *Testimony to the Truth and Friendship Commission on Rape and Sexual Violence in the context of the Popular Consultation in East Timor 1999*, March 2007.

LIBERIA: Towards the end of the five-year civil war, which ran from 1999 to 2003, 49 per cent of women between the ages of fifteen and seventy reported experiencing at least one act of physical or sexual violence at the hands of a soldier or fighter. See Shana Swiss and others, "Violence against women during the Liberian civil conflict," *Journal of the American Medical Association* 279 (1998): 625–29.

CENTRAL AFRICAN REPUBLIC: Between 2002 and 2003, more than 1,000 documented cases of rape were committed by the Presidential Guard and the National Army. See Katy Glassborow, "CAR case to focus on sexual violence," *Institute for War and Peace Reporting*, May 24, 2007.

BURUNDI: Between November 2004 and November 2007, the Seruka centre of Médecins Sans Frontières Belgium registered 5,466 cases of sexual violence, an average of 1,366 victims a year and 27 victims a week. See ACAT Burundi and OMCT, *NGO Report on Violence Against Women in Burundi (CEDAW, 40th Session): Executive Summary* (Geneva, 2008), p. 3.

UGANDA: At least 60 per cent of women in Pabbo camp, the largest camp for internally displaced people in war-torn northern Uganda, have encountered some form of sexual and domestic violence. See Akumu Christine Okot, Amony Isabella and Otim Gerald, *Suffering in Silence: A Study of Sexual and Gender Based Violence (SGBV) in Pabbo Camp, Gulu District, Northern Uganda* (New York: UNICEF, 2005), p. 9.

DARFUR: Rape and sexual violence have been used in Darfur by government forces and government-backed Janjaweed militias as a deliberate strategy to terrorize the population. See Amnesty International, *Five Years On: No Justice for Sexual Violence in Darfur* (London, 2008). Between October 2004 and February 2005, Médecins Sans Frontières treated approximately 500 rape victims in Darfur, though the total number of women raped is likely much higher. Médecins Sans Frontières, *The Crushing Burden of Rape: Sexual Violence in Darfur—A Briefing Paper by Médecins Sans Frontières* (Amsterdam, 2005), p. 2.

KENYA: Kenya has experienced a 7,500 per cent increase in the incidence of sexual violence against women in the aftermath of the post-election crisis, December 2007–June 2008, with a catastrophic breakdown in health system support for rape victims. See Kyle Kinner, "A Paradigm Shift in Prevention," *Caucus for Evidence-Based Prevention Newsletter* 13 (2008):1.

2

TESTIMONIALS

MARIE LOUISE NIYOBUHUNGIRO

BORN: 1975 (day and month unknown) *

BIRTHPLACE: Shyorongi, just outside Kigali

P EOPLE THINK I am crazy because I am always crying, and I do not blame them for thinking so. I am always angry, and I do not sleep at night. I hoped secretly that I would die during the genocide, but being among other survivors within a survivors' organization has brought me comfort and hope. I feel like I have a family now, and I am very grateful for that.

Before the genocide, we were a family of eight children—five girls and three boys. I was the fourth child in the family. My father was a teacher, and my mother was a farmer. We lived in Shyorongi, just outside Kigali. There were many Tutsi families in Shyorongi; we had only one Hutu neighbour. Although he was our neighbour, that Hutu hated us, especially my father, because we were Tutsi. In 1991, my father was poisoned, and I suspect that the Hutu neighbour who hated him so much did it. When my father started to feel sick, he went to a traditional clinic. After his death, my mother asked the people at the clinic what my father had died of, and they told her that he had been poisoned. Today, our former Hutu neighbour and all his family are in prison for crimes they committed during the genocide.

Our mother told us that, in 1959, another Hutu had set fire to my mother's house and then accused my father of doing it. When my mother told us

---

* Some Rwandans do not know their specific birth date because the dates are not recorded, especially in rural areas.

her history of discrimination for being Tutsi, she would also tell us not to dismiss it as a tale. And years later, what we thought to be just a part of history became our reality.

On April 6, 1994, when President Habyarimana died, the local authorities ordered my family to go back to our house. We had been walking outside. But we did not feel secure in our house, and we went to pass the night on our cassava plantation instead. The next morning, we went to our uncle's house, which was about a thirty-minute walk from our house. The Interahamwe surrounded my uncle's house a few hours later. As the killings hadn't started yet, the militia were just trying to frighten us. When the Interahamwe got tired of this and left, we ran to the Catholic church of Mboza, which was about fifteen minutes' walking distance from my uncle's house. Almost three hundred Tutsi had found refuge in the church.

We arrived at the church at about ten in the morning, and a few minutes later the Interahamwe and FAR soldiers started shooting. They had guns and shot all the men, including my uncle. I fell, and some dead bodies fell on top of me. I was all covered with blood. I heard screams and babies crying, but I was unconscious for most of the time the attack was continuing. The next day, they came back to kill those who were not yet dead. There was blood all over me, and the killers thought that I was dead, too, so they left me there, lying among those dead bodies. Once I had regained consciousness, all I could see were a lot of bodies lying around the church. The stench of blood was thick in the air. Except for one of my sisters, all my other relatives died during this attack at the church. Out of three hundred people in the church, only five had survived. I felt completely empty. I had no thoughts and felt nothing, nothing at all.

After the Interahamwe left the second time, I left the church. My sister and I went in different directions, because we felt that even if one of us was killed, the other one might have a chance to survive. I fled in the direction of a nearby forest and ran into an Interahamwe on the road, who asked me where I came from. I recognized him as a fellow churchgoer named Ntirenganya. I told him that I had lost my way and was just wandering around. He said that he had finished killing for the day, so others would kill me, not him.

After that close encounter, I spent three days hiding in the bushes. On the fourth day, I went to the house of another uncle, who had not yet had

Marie Louise at home with her children

an opportunity to flee, because his wife had just given birth. He and his wife had already been warned by their neighbour, an Interahamwe, to leave their house immediately; they would not have much longer to live otherwise. Together with my uncle's relatives, I left his house that night. But, at the gate in front of his house, we ran into a group of Interahamwe militia. They took the girls among us and brought us to a nearby roadblock in order to kill us.

Every FAR soldier or Interahamwe we met on the way made an insulting speech or had a rod to beat us with. One of them said that the girls should be brought to the Twa, who were often ridiculed in Rwanda and considered stupid and worthless. At some point, a FAR soldier picked me out of the group and took me to a nearby bush. I don't know what happened to the other girls I was with.

This soldier raped me. After he was done with me, he took me to a house and told the owners of the house to keep me safe, so that he could rape me every time he came. He told them if anything happened to me he would kill them. Every time he came to the house after that, he took me to the forest to rape me. Over five days, I was raped five times a day. The rapist didn't say anything to me. In the forest, the local people often saw me being raped by this man. The local people, an Interahamwe militiaman and other Hutu would watch the soldier rape me and did not even raise their little finger to stop it. They didn't care, because I was Tutsi. They were silent. The FAR soldier who did this to me was so old—about forty—and so savage. It was the very first time I saw what a man was capable of doing.

After those five days, the old man brought me to a lady called Mukandoli, who was an Interahamwe too, and I stayed there. She didn't care about my situation. She didn't say anything, except when she sometimes ordered me to go out and farm. I stayed with this lady for one week. Then another FAR soldier came and told Mukandoli that his colonel wanted me.

When I arrived at the FAR camp, the colonel had the "manners" to ask me if I wanted to sleep with him. But I knew that whatever answer I gave, the outcome would be the same, and that I would end up in his bed if he had one. I said no and ran into the bushes. His soldiers spent the whole night looking for me, but they didn't find me.

A little later, I saw a house and entered it. The house appeared to be an Interahamwe's harem, full of Tutsi women and girls. There were about ten teenage girls in the house, all between about sixteen and twenty years old. The FAR soldiers who were looking for me found me there and took me back to the colonel. On the way back, they asked me to sleep with them. I told them I could do that the next day. While they were still discussing this, I managed to escape, and I walked all the way to Ruhengeri, which was already under the control of the RPF.

For two weeks, I hid myself during the day and walked during the night. I ate nothing and hid in the bushes. When the RPF went to Kigali, I followed them. I walked just behind them, back to my place of birth. I occupied a house that belonged to owners who had fled the country, because my family house had been destroyed during the genocide. To make a living, I dug the fields for a farmer. Later, a fund for survivors was established, which provided me with a bit of support. I lost four brothers and sisters during the genocide, and one sister died of kidney failure right afterwards.

Before the genocide, I had never been intimate with a man, and yet now I have gotten to know many without my consent. Even after the genocide, in 2000, a neighbour came to my house, forced my door open and raped me. There was no use screaming, because no one lived close by. I became pregnant as a result of this rape, and the child died immediately upon birth. The doctors then pressured me to take an HIV test, and I discovered I am HIV positive.

I live in very bad conditions because I didn't go to school. I have no job and am too weak now to dig the fields. I get food from an organization that helps me to survive. I have had four children since the genocide, all from different fathers. The father of one of my children is a neighbour, and the others have jobs in the neighbourhood. I never see them. I only had sex with each of them once. Luckily, my oldest three children are not HIV positive, but my youngest child has not been tested yet. I wish I could give my children some more support, including buying them school materials and clothes. I am always sick, sometimes because of HIV and other times because of the beatings I endured during the genocide. I was hit on my knees and head with a club and I suffer from severe headaches now.

I don't think I can forgive the FAR soldiers or the Interahamwe. I don't want to hear about reconciliation. I accused them in the *gacaca* courts, including the one who raped me, those who participated in the killings in the church and those I saw at the roadblock, but now they are being released. *Gacaca* courts do not bring justice. I think the best punishment those men could get is the death penalty, because they killed others, too. We need justice. The *génocidaires* should not be released. I shared my testimony in order to help establish justice, and I hope it will do that.

MARIE ODETTE KAYITESI

BORN: September 8, 1969
BIRTHPLACE: Runyinya, Butare

I NEVER KNEW OF the word "genocide" before the day I saw the genocide with my own eyes. During the genocide in Rwanda, I endured so much and wondered why I existed. I hated the world and asked myself whether there was a god. If he really existed, how could he allow these atrocities to happen?

I spent my childhood in Gikongoro, my mother's birthplace. Our family owned cows and land there. My father was a teacher, but he had retired from teaching by the time the genocide began. My mother was a housewife, and she took care of my seven brothers and sisters and me. When I first went to school, I studied at private schools because the discrimination against Tutsi in public schools was unbearable. However, private school fees became very expensive, and I could not continue my secondary studies there. So I attended a public Catholic school in Kigali, where I lived with my older sister Dorothy, who was married to a Tutsi man. I studied in Kigali because the community in Gikongoro knew my family, and my ethnicity was always mentioned in my school file there. Including students' ethnicity in school files was a way for teachers to discriminate against Tutsi. In Kigali I met my fiancé, Xavier, who was our neighbour. We were engaged for two years before the genocide began.

When the president's plane crashed, I was living with Dorothy in Muhima, a neighbourhood in Kigali. Two days later, on the morning of April 8, we heard the screams of Tutsi who were being shot by Interahamwe. That same morning, the Interahamwe approached Dorothy's house, but we managed to escape, taking different routes. I hid in Dorothy's outdoor toilet. From there I could see my neighbour's children gesturing to me to hide at their house. My neighbour was an old Hutu woman named Marcelline, who was friendly with Xavier's sister. So I fled to Marcelline's house, where Xavier also happened to be hiding. There I spent a week hiding with Xavier and two others, a Tutsi boy and woman who sought refuge with Marcelline.

After a week, a group of Interahamwe approached Marcelline's house. They were led by none other than Nkezabera, a man who owned the house that Xavier was renting before the genocide. The militia had searched every house in the quarter and finally arrived at the house we were hiding in. They ordered Marcelline to show them the cockroaches she was hiding. Marcelline said she didn't have any cockroaches in her house, but her son Aimable, who also lived there, told her to let the militia enter if she didn't want all of them, including her children, to be killed too. Aimable had been kind to us, but I knew he wanted us to leave his house. Marcelline finally relented and let the militia in. They found all four of us cowering in a room and ordered us outside.

Once we emerged from the house, the Interahamwe descended on Xavier and beat him all over his body with every weapon they had. They targeted Xavier because they thought he was an RPF spy who planned to help the RPF take over Kigali. They suspected him of this because he had volunteered with the RPF before the genocide. The Interahamwe slashed his head with machetes, bludgeoned him with clubs and sawed off his legs. While they were busy with Xavier, they seemed to have forgotten about Marcelline and me, so we inched away slowly until we were behind her house. From there, we could watch what was happening without being noticed. Xavier screamed in a very high-pitched voice while they were sawing off his legs, and I felt an indescribable hurt in my heart at that same moment.

Three hours later, a man in an Interahamwe truck who was removing bodies from the streets passed by and left Xavier lying where he was. I think the man left Xavier lying there because he was not yet dead. Later, a Red Cross truck commandeered by another Interahamwe passed by, and one of the men inside it said, while pointing at Xavier, that he was "not yet finished." Xavier replied very weakly that he had always hated humiliation. That same man got off the truck and hit Xavier on the head with an axe, which finally killed him. The Tutsi boy who was hiding at Marcelline's witnessed all of this and told me about it later.

I continued to hide in Marcelline's house. Two weeks after Xavier's death, another group of Interahamwe, which this time included Marcelline's son Aimable, returned to the house. They ordered Marcelline to release her cockroach. She refused, but they threatened her, saying they would kill her too if she did not cooperate. Marcelline was about to argue with them when I came forward and revealed myself. I didn't want Marcelline to be killed because of me.

The Interahamwe took me to a little house not far from Marcelline's place. They were all very dirty and looked like bandits. I didn't recognize any of them. When we got to the little house, one of them removed my clothes. When I was completely naked, he asked his mates who was going to be the first. A fight between them then ensued, because everyone wanted to be the first on me. In the end, one of the Interahamwe, who looked to me like a homeless man, pushed me on the floor and went on me. After he was finished, another one came. I remember at least ten of them on me, but I don't know the exact number of those who followed, because I fell unconscious after that.

Almost all of them looked homeless. Now, whenever I pass through the area where I was raped, I see men on the street looking at me in a particular way, and I ask myself if any of the men who raped me are among those staring at me. What saddens me most is that the men who raped me are walking freely in the streets today and have never been held accountable.

When I regained consciousness, the Interahamwe were discussing how to kill me. One of the men, named Cyimana, said that he would take me to his house and make me his sex slave, because I was still beautiful. Cyimana then took me to Marcelline's house and told her to take good care of me, because he would be coming to retrieve his "property" any time he wanted. When Marcelline saw me she didn't seem too pleased. I think she feared I would be killed in her house. However, out of compassion, she washed me with warm water, because I was still aching terribly. When I started to feel better, she went to the nearest roadblock, which was under the supervision of a well-known, rich Hutu man named Kamanayo, and begged Kamanayo to hide me in his compound, saying that I was distantly related to his Tutsi wife, who had died before the genocide. This wasn't really true; I just happened to be from the same province as his wife. Still, he accepted, and Marcelline took me to his compound when it got dark.

At Kamanayo's compound, I met an old Tutsi woman who had begun renting a house there after having been chased out of her own house by her Hutu husband. I got to know Kamanayo a little better while hiding in his compound. He was an old man who did not kill anyone during the genocide. No one was killed at the roadblock he was responsible for, either. While he was not cruel to me, he was not kind, either. I stayed in his compound for one month.

While I was hiding at Kamanayo's compound, I heard that Cyimana, the Interahamwe to whom I "belonged," got very angry when he didn't find me at Marcelline's house and spent days hunting for me. He didn't know where I was hiding. Kamanayo told me that Cyimana planned to kill me on the date all Tutsi in Rwanda were to be executed—the last day of the mourning period for President Habyarimana, three months after his death. I was scared, but soon my fears were allayed. The RPF arrived in Kigali the day before the Tutsi execution date. Very early in the morning, Kamanayo woke the old Tutsi woman and me and told us to flee, because the government had lost the war.

As we left Kamanayo's compound, we met a small group of Interahamwe in front of his house. I ran and took my own route. While I ran, I could see Interahamwe all around me killing Tutsi. When I stopped for a short break, I encountered a young man who asked me who I was fleeing from. When I told him that the Interahamwe were pursuing me, he comforted me and said that everything was under control. The young man took me to a hotel in Kigali, where a group of survivors had gathered, among them recent widows and orphans. The survivors were wounded all over their bodies, and some of them were still bleeding. I found out that the young man was with the RPF. At the hotel, RPF soldiers told us that they knew we had lost our loved ones, but that we had to be strong and live on. I stayed there for two weeks. The RPF soldiers then informed us that the genocide was over and said we should return to our houses.

When I left the hotel, I went to live in Xavier's old house. No one was inside the house anymore, but it contained a lot of furniture that had been

Marie Odette at home with her two children and an orphaned child *(far left)* she cares for

stolen from Tutsi houses. The Interahamwe leader, Nkezabera, stored his loot there. As people slowly returned to their homes, I learned from neighbours that my older sister Dorothy had been killed with her family during the genocide. The neighbours didn't know how she had been killed, though. In August, I made a trip back to Gikongoro to find out what had happened to my family. There, I learned that my entire family had been killed.

After the genocide, I worked in a prison stockroom. On the bus to work one day, I met a young man from the north of Rwanda, a university student. He fell in love with me, but he kept pressing me about whether I had been raped during the genocide. I always denied that I was. He said that if my health was fine, we could live together. After two years of living together,

I became pregnant with our first child. During my pregnancy, I became ill and went to the hospital, where I told the doctor I had been raped. He advised me to take an HIV test. I took the test, but I did not receive the results.

After I gave birth to my second child, I had another blood test. I did not receive the results of that test, either. Then I became very ill. While I was ill, my boyfriend abandoned me. I went to see the doctor, and only then did he reveal to me that I was HIV positive. The other doctors in the hospital were angry with my doctor for not giving me my results immediately. All hope abandoned me then as I realized that my life was going to be cut short.

After my boyfriend abandoned me, my children and I lived in very bad conditions. I heard about organizations that provided comfort and support and I started attending counselling sessions at one organization, which also provided me with antiretroviral medication and food. There I met women who faced the same problems I did. Whenever we shared our problems, I felt better. Today, I live with my two children. Thankfully, they are not HIV positive. My children make me very happy, but the thought that they will be alone when I am gone breaks my heart.

No one has ever asked for my forgiveness, and I do not forgive the Interahamwe who hurt me. Nkezabera, one of the Interahamwe who murdered Xavier, offered me 100,000 Rwandan francs so I would not testify against him in the *gacaca* court. I told him that no money in the world could replace the loss I still have in my heart. Nkezabera was eventually convicted at the *gacaca* court and sentenced to five years. However, he has since appealed the case, after bribing the panel of judges for a shorter sentence. Even if I felt like forgiving, it is not easy, because those Interahamwe continue to lie during their trials.

I have shared my testimony here so that the world may know what really happened in Rwanda. So much pain still lives inside of us, and the fact that most of us live with HIV makes things worse. I live in poor conditions, and I do not have money to pay for my children's school fees. I wonder what will happen to my children when I am dead. I hope people will reach out and help them. I pray that the truth about the genocide will one day be revealed. Genocide is a vicious cycle. I hope the world ensures that genocide never happens again, because I want a bright future for my children and I never want them to endure what I have.

MARIE JEANNE MUREKATETE

BORN: July 1971 (day unknown)
BIRTHPLACE: Gafunzo (now Nyamasheke), Cyangugu

I WAS BORN IN Gafunzo, a large commune in Cyangugu Prefecture in the southwest of Rwanda. When I was eleven, my father was poisoned by our Hutu neighbours. He died, and my mother had to raise eight children all by herself. Because the Hutu in our community were poor and my family owned a lot of property, the Hutu were our labourers. They were very jealous of my family, and I think that is why they poisoned my father. We were able to survive after my father's death because he left us cows and land and my brother was a rich merchant.

Perhaps I was naïve, but when I was young, I felt that all ethnic groups lived in harmony. I had a very happy childhood. Only rarely did I feel as if I didn't belong. I never felt there was any reason to hate the Hutu. The only time I felt upset was at school. When both Hutu and Tutsi passed their exams, the teachers, who were all Hutu, favoured Hutu students. I hated my teachers. Even though I was clever, I could not succeed.

I met my husband through my brother. In 1992, he asked for my hand in marriage and I accepted. We were so happy together. We lived in Gafunzo, but quite a distance from my parents' house. My husband was a merchant who sold sugar and rice. Soon after we were married, I gave birth to a beautiful baby girl.

On the morning of April 7, 1994, my father-in-law came to tell us that President Habyarimana had died in a plane crash and that his guards had

41

started killing Tutsi. We decided to stay put, and my husband went to work as usual. Two days later, on the evening of April 9, my in-laws learned that my husband had been killed by the Interahamwe while leaving his store. I was devastated. My in-laws decided to flee to the Congo, so I was left all alone with my daughter. I decided to go to my parents' house, which was about five hours away on foot.

As I approached my parents' house with my daughter, I could see Interahamwe burning the house and killing cows. I could also see, from a short distance away, that my mother was hiding in our cornfield, waiting for the killers to leave. My mother pointed towards the church in nearby Shangi and gestured for me to run. I found out later that all my brothers and sisters had already gone there, on the Interahamwe militia's instructions. This was part of the militia's strategy: to group all Tutsi together in one place so we were easier to kill.

My mother hadn't gone to the church with the others, because she wanted to pack some food to take with her. After the militia eventually left and she was making her way to the church, she was detained by a group of Interahamwe, who cut her ear off. They gave my mother her ear and told her to show it to the others at the church as a symbol of the eventual fate of the Tutsi. They also said that while the Hutu were merely looting at first, they would soon progress to killing. My mother was released to be a messenger for those threats. She fled to the church, where we were reunited.

Two days after I got there, the Interahamwe militia entered the church and dragged away some of our men to be killed. This continued for two weeks. Then a militia leader named Yusufu entered the church with several Interahamwe, and they spent the entire day massacring Tutsi: it didn't matter if we were men, women or children. I hid under some dead bodies to fool the killers into thinking I was also dead. My baby was still on my back at the time. While I lay in hiding, I could see the militia killing people all around me by stabbing them with knives and hacking them with machetes. I wasn't scared, though; I just felt confused. Some people managed to escape through a hole in the wall. Eventually I fell unconscious. When I finally awoke, I thought my baby would probably be dead. But fortunately she had survived the night with me.

When it got dark, I escaped from the church with my daughter. I discovered my beautiful eighteen-year-old cousin, Liberatha, in the bushes where

we were both hiding. We decided to head towards the nearby football stadium because we had heard there was no killing there. A number of people at the church had come from the stadium, which they said French soldiers were protecting. Liberatha and I walked in the rain. We were so exhausted that we stopped to rest in some bushes beside a river. Liberatha was breathing with great pain and difficulty. When we heard footsteps, I fled to hide in another bush with my baby. Liberatha ran in a different direction, and she was caught by a Hutu man who raped her there. I could see everything from where I was hiding.

I decided to run before the Hutu man discovered me. While I was running, I realized my baby must be very hungry, and I remembered an old Hutu lady, a friend of my father's, who lived nearby. I thought that she could probably hide us for a little while. I went to her house, and she gave us some food and drinks. A few hours later, though, the Interahamwe arrived and interrogated me about my ethnic group, what I was doing there and whether I had my identity card. I told them I had no identity card and didn't know what my ethnic group was. They told me to return to my house to fetch my identity card, because they didn't believe me. Still, they couldn't be sure, since they didn't know me, so they let me go. The old lady told me it was a trick and said the militia would kill me if I returned to her house with my card. Instead, I headed to the stadium with my baby.

As I made my way towards the stadium, I could see that it was surrounded by Interahamwe, French soldiers, roadblocks and what seemed like thousands of corpses. I saw a child among the dead bodies and realized it was my cousin Marcel, who was fourteen at the time. He was bleeding from a cut to the head. I lay down among the corpses next to Marcel, with my baby still on my back. I didn't think there was anywhere else I could go. While I lay next to Marcel, he became unconscious. After about an hour, I saw a Red Cross vehicle full of *bazungu*, white people, approaching. I yelled at them for help, but they didn't speak Kinyarwanda, so they didn't stop until I pointed at Marcel. When they saw that he was still alive, they took him into their car and gave me some biscuits. The Interahamwe did not notice all this happening, because they were busy killing other people. Even though the Red Cross witnessed the crimes the Interahamwe were committing, they were powerless to stop them. All they could do was search among the bodies to treat those who were still alive.

After the Red Cross vehicle left, I went to hide in a small forest near the stadium. I climbed a tree with my baby on my back. Then I got the idea of going to my older sister's house; she had married a Hutu man, and I thought that he could protect us. On my way there, I came across a roadblock with many corpses. There were Interahamwe at the roadblock, and they interrogated me about where I was going. I acted like a madwoman as I told them I was going to my older sister's house. They asked me how I was going to get there and suggested I wait for my sister's son to come pick me up.

Throughout the interrogation, I denied that I was Tutsi. But the militia said they knew that my older sister was a Tutsi and that I must be one too. Eventually, one of the Interahamwe said he knew where my sister's house was and would take me there. Instead, he took me to a narrow ditch, where he took my baby from my back. He threw me in the ditch and raped me. Afterward, he said he would take me to my sister's house, but I was hysterical and too exhausted to walk. Seeing this, he cried, "Why should I take you? You're already dead!" He abandoned me there, and I spent two days in that ditch. During that time, my daughter rolled into the ditch beside me, so I was able to hold her next to me and breastfeed her.

On the evening of the second night, I left the ditch. I could see militia in a nearby forest. I avoided their torches and crossed the small forest to get back to the stadium, all the time with my daughter on my back. At the stadium, the Interahamwe were drunk, rowdy and eating meat. I managed to enter, because it was dark and the killers could not see that I was Tutsi. In the stadium, I was reunited with some relatives who had thought I was already dead. I was elated to see them and no longer felt scared of death. My older sister was there, too. My relatives gave me some food that the Red Cross had been distributing. I learned from them that the man who had raped my cousin Liberatha had taken her to his house. Some other Tutsi at the stadium had seen Liberatha being abducted.

Although we spent a month in that stadium, life was not safe. The Interahamwe would enter the stadium with lists of the names of educated Tutsi, call those people out and remove them from among us. Anyone who could speak French or English was on a list. The French soldiers stationed outside the stadium knew what was going on. The people who were taken never returned. We wondered what had happened to them, but we were also distracted by other things, especially our hunger. We were all famished, and we resorted to eating anything we could get our hands on—even dirt. Though the Red Cross distributed food at the stadium, the Interahamwe would seize it and keep it for themselves.

After a month of hunger and imprisonment, people in the stadium rebelled, and many fled. It was chaos. The Interahamwe ran after and shot many of those who fled, all while the French were watching. Those who ran first were killed immediately. I also ran from the stadium. When the shooting began, I ran back with others, though I was very weak.

After another week, the French soldiers loaded us into a vehicle to take us to Nyarushishi camp in the Zone Turquoise in Cyangugu. The camp was very far away from the stadium. Those of us with radios heard that the RPF had taken over almost all of Rwanda, except for the area where this camp was located. I suspect the French soldiers knew the RPF soldiers were approaching fast and wanted to take us somewhere we could be easily killed.

At Nyarushishi camp, I saw French soldiers picking up girls and young women to take back to their own camps. The girls and young women who were taken did not return, and the few who did had only two words to say: "Ni *abafaransa*," meaning "It is the French people." The French soldiers routinely gave biscuits and candies to children so that the children would show them where to find young women. It became very common for the French to come to the camp at night looking for women.

At the camp, the UNHCR, the United Nations High Commissioner for Refugees, brought us food. But we also needed firewood, so after a week I went to the little forest in Nyarushishi with some other women and my baby. I collected firewood in the forest some distance away from the other women. Suddenly, a French soldier appeared out of nowhere, grabbed me by the arm, took me to a trench, took my baby off my back, slapped me, pushed me into the trench and raped me, while five other French soldiers watched. I thought he was going to kill me, so I didn't shout or scream. He behaved like a wild animal. When he finished raping me, the others raped me too, one by one until all six had had their fill. They did to me whatever perversion came to their minds. I felt so sick and weak that I couldn't move. I couldn't have screamed even if I wanted to, because they put their tongues in my mouth. After they were finished, they threw my baby on top of me in the trench. My vagina felt completely destroyed.

The six French soldiers left me there, and I spent the night in the trench. The next day, several old women discovered me and carried me to a Red

Cross clinic at the camp. I communicated only with gestures, because I was not able to speak properly. I didn't tell anyone that the French had raped me, especially not the Red Cross, because they were *bazungu* and I worried they might have been French too.

After that, there was no escaping the French soldiers. They came into the camp looking for women to rape. Once my vagina had healed, I was raped in the camp by French soldiers four more times. I don't know if they were the same ones who had raped me before, because I have a hard time distinguishing the faces of *bazungu*. The soldiers were not ashamed of raping women in front of children and elders. It became a nightly routine. But no one dared to speak out, because we were all scared of what the French soldiers would do to us.

After we had endured these horrible conditions at the camp for a month, soldiers from Chad arrived. They said they were from a UN peacekeeping operation called UNAMIR, the UN Assistance Mission for Rwanda. Once the UNAMIR soldiers arrived, the French soldiers stopped raping us. The soldiers from Chad watched over us and gave us biscuits to eat. We were freed by advancing RPF soldiers a month later, in August. When they arrived, we danced and sang that we were free at last.

The RPF instructed us to return to our homes. I knew all the houses in Gafunzo had been burned and destroyed, so I went instead to nearby Kamembe with my daughter. Kamembe was a small town in Cyangugu where the houses were still standing because they were all inhabited by Hutu. Other people from the camp went to Rusizi, on the Congolese border, but I suspected the Interahamwe would raid the area at night to kill any survivors. In Kamembe I reunited with my older sister. She had fled to the Congo during the genocide with her Hutu husband but now had returned to Kamembe.

In Kamembe, my sister rented a house for me and gave me some money so that I could start a business selling fruits and vegetables. I soon learned that both my brother and my mother had been killed during the Shangi church massacre. My brother, who was shot while trying to escape from the church, had fled to my parents' house, where he hid in an outhouse. This didn't deter the Interahamwe. A militia member pursued my brother, slashed him with his machete and threw him down the latrine.

While life was better in Kamembe, we did not feel secure until RPF soldiers were permanently posted at the Rwandan borders. After some time there, I met a young RPF soldier named Gaspard, who asked me to marry him. He said that I was still young and had the right to a good life. I married him, and we moved in together in Kamembe. Soon I was pregnant, but my husband was sent to the Congo. RPF soldiers there were battling the Interahamwe who had fled Rwanda upon the RPF's arrival. When our daughter was born in 1997, my husband ensured that all of his salary was transferred to me. Gaspard returned from battle eight months later, and we moved to Kigali, where I met his family. I continued to sell fruits and vegetables there.

My husband was a good man, and he really comforted me after all I had been through. I felt life was worth living again. We had another child, a boy, in 2002. Gaspard helped me to raise my oldest daughter and some orphans I was caring for. But he eventually fell ill with a brain tumour. At the military hospital, he was diagnosed with HIV. I decided to be tested, too, and that is when I found out I was also HIV positive. Gaspard died in 2004, and I miss him terribly.

My children are unhappy. People beat them and make fun of them because I am HIV positive. We are so poor. I have been unable to continue my business, because I must use any money I have to pay for treatment. Before my husband died, he brought money home. Now my children are unhappy because they have nothing. I wish so much to give them new things—clothing, school materials, anything—but I do not have the means. Fortunately, my children were not infected with the virus, and recently I have been supported by charities who give me medicine to treat the HIV. Other widows and orphans have comforted me when I was in mourning and brought joy and laughter into my life when my heart was filled with pain and sorrow. I am now feeling less lonely and more secure.

I don't feel hatred towards the Hutu. I have never accused those who killed my family at the *gacaca* courts, because that won't do anything for me. The killers can't bring my family back, so I don't see any point in accusing them. I do have advice for others who suffer: as a genocide survivor who is HIV positive, has lost two husbands and is responsible for four children, I think anyone who has travelled the same road as I have should pray and be patient. Just be patient.

JEANETTE UWIMANA

BORN: April 2, 1972

BIRTHPLACE: Nyarugenge quarter, Kigali

BEFORE THE GENOCIDE, my father, my sister and I lived in Butare, but in 1978 we were forced to move to Kigali. My father was not safe in Butare; he could not spend more than a month without going to prison, because he was Tutsi. Since 1959, his identity card had been regularly checked for his ethnicity, especially upon his return from Burundi, where he met my mother. My mother, a businesswoman, had gone back to Burundi. She refused to stay in Rwanda because of the discrimination Tutsi faced. My father was lucky to find a good job at the National Bank in Kigali. People initially did not know that we were Tutsi, and we thought we would be safe there. But in 1990, when the RPF tried to invade Rwanda, my father was accused of being an RPF spy and was fired from the bank. He went to prison for two months.

I married Diogene on November 28, 1990. He was a friend of my cousin, and we had met for the first time at my cousin's house, while my father was still in prison. Very quickly, I became pregnant, so we decided to get married. I stopped attending secondary school because of my pregnancy, after having completed only two years. We found a house to rent in Nyarugenge quarter in Kigali. My husband, who was also Tutsi, owned a bar, and I was a merchant in the market, where I sold rice, sugar, fruit and powdered milk. We also had some land in Shyorongi, a village near Kigali that was my husband's birthplace. There we were building a house, which we planned to live in once it was finished. We grew potatoes, beans, bananas and cassava

there, and we ate this produce ourselves or gave it to our parents. Sometimes we sold it to neighbours.

We had a very good life. Even though our neighbours were almost all Hutu, that didn't seem to be a problem. In the beginning our neighbours didn't know we were Tutsi, but when the multi-party system was introduced in Rwanda in the early 1990s, they found out that my husband belonged to the P.L. party, which was composed mostly of Tutsi. We had two beautiful children, a daughter and a son. In 1994, our daughter was three years old and our son only three months old.

On the evening of April 6, 1994, our daughter was staying at her grandparents' house. My brother-in-law was staying temporarily at our house, preparing for his exams. My husband and I didn't have a chance to listen to the radio, because our power had been cut off. The Presidential Guards were at our front door the next morning, though, and while we were still wondering about what was happening, they forced us to leave our house and to show them our identity cards, which specified our ethnicity. A large crowd of Tutsi and Hutu had gathered in the street, and the Presidential Guards told Tutsi to go to one side of the street and Hutu to another. I knew exactly what was about to follow for Tutsi, so I threw my identity card away. The Interahamwe shouted that they were killing the *inyenzi*—the cockroaches—and the guards went to see what was happening. We took that opportunity to return to our house, where we tried to come up with an escape strategy.

While we were still thinking through all the possibilities, the Interahamwe came to our house and took my husband with them, without explaining why. He never came back. I don't know how he was killed or where the remains of his body are, but one of my neighbours told me afterwards that he must have been killed, because she saw one of the Interahamwe wearing my husband's jacket. About two hours later, at around ten-thirty in the morning, the militia returned. They accused my brother-in-law of being an RPF spy and took him with them. The Interahamwe came back yet again at around one in the afternoon. This time, they took me to a hall where Tutsi were being killed. They beat me with their guns until a policeman who was a friend of my husband's begged them for mercy in order to spare my life. This helped, and they told me to go back home. I did, since I didn't know where else I could go.

I felt very lonely, and I hated myself. I felt responsible for what had happened to my family. Right before the militia took my husband away, they told us that all our other relatives, including our daughter, had been killed. The wife of the leader of a militia group—a woman who had gone to school with my husband and who knew many people—had betrayed them to the Interahamwe. My baby son and I were still alive, but I felt that I should have died along with my husband, my daughter and my other relatives.

That same day, five Interahamwe came to my house and ordered me to show them all the guns I had. I told them that I did not have a gun, because I was not a soldier. One of them pushed me into the bedroom and said that I would be a good replacement for a gun. He threw me on the bed and tore off my clothes. He raped me while his mates pointed their guns at me. After he was finished, another one raped me, and then another, until all five had had their way with me. Eventually they left, saying that their "work" was calling them. Killing Tutsi was their "work." I hated myself and considered myself less than a human being. I thought that those who had died were in a better position than I.

My private parts were aching and bleeding profusely. Four days after the rapes, one of my neighbours, a Hutu female friend, found the courage to come into my house. All of my neighbours had seen or heard what had happened to me. She came regularly after that, comforted me, brought me some food, helped me to wash myself and the baby and gave the baby some milk. My neighbour urged me to escape, but I was afraid I would be killed no matter where I went, so I decided to stay in my house. I gave some money to this woman so that she could cook food for me at her own house and bring it to us.

Two weeks later, a large group of Interahamwe militia came into our area and commanded everyone to leave their houses. I had no identity card anymore, and I took my time putting my baby on my back. One of the Interahamwe entered the house and said if I gave him some money he might spare my life. I gave him all the money I had, and he left me in my sitting room.

Apparently this man's militia friends asked him why he had only demanded money from this rich woman. They told him that he should also rape me. Some hours later, he returned with other Interahamwe. They raped me in my sitting room, saying that they had not spared me for nothing.

Jeanette and her children at home near Kigali

This continued for two months, practically every day. The rapists were mostly Presidential Guards, but also Interahamwe militia and FAR soldiers. They were all very brutal; the Interahamwe most brutal of all. The Interahamwe would rape me wherever in the house they found me. Sometimes the rapists came alone, sometimes in a group. Often they came both in the mornings and in the evenings. They also told others about the possibility of raping me. They would cruelly ask where my husband was and threaten to kill me later. They called me a snake and said that it was the end for all snakes. I was regularly beaten. This whole time, a policeman kept assuring me that the RPF were getting closer. He also advised me to keep myself dirty, not to wash myself, so that I would not attract the rapists. Although this policeman was decent with me, two other policemen raped me.

During this period, I felt like I was no longer a human being, and I wanted to kill myself. But I couldn't do it, since I still had my son to care for. Eventually I no longer felt pain; instead, I felt like a ghost. I didn't really think about escaping, since I felt I would be killed either way. There was no one to help me, and I preferred to die in my own house. This nightmare ended the day the Inkotanyi arrived, July 4, 1994.

As the Inkotanyi were approaching, the Interahamwe tried to kill all the remaining Tutsi, and they forced me to flee Kigali with them. I remember seeing a girl who tried to escape. She was immediately stabbed to death, so I didn't try to follow her example. We marched northwest towards the DRC, the Democratic Republic of Congo. There was a lot of panic. When I arrived in Gisenyi, someone offered me a ride to Kibuye for five thousand Rwandan francs. I thought it would be safer in Kibuye for my baby and me, as I had heard from other survivors who had returned from Goma, in the DRC, that Hutu were killing Tutsi there. Congolese soldiers were also killing Tutsi in the DRC because the Interahamwe had told the Congolese that the Tutsi were rich. Those who tried to cross into the DRC had their belongings taken away by the Congolese. Every time Tutsi tried to cross the border, the Congolese soldiers asked them for money. If they didn't have any, or didn't hand over what they had, they were killed. I decided that I would rather die in my own country, so I paid the driver the five thousand francs to take me to Kibuye.

Upon my arrival in Kibuye, I tried to find a house to stay in. It was very difficult, because there were dead bodies everywhere, and they had started to rot and smelled terrible. I finally found a school in the centre of Kibuye that did not contain any rotting bodies. It was very hard, because I was sharing the room with the Interahamwe and I could not do anything about it. Although the Interahamwe were still killing people in Kibuye, they only killed those they were certain were Tutsi. They didn't know that I was Tutsi. During the period I stayed in the school, I had no time to think about myself, because my baby was sick and vomiting all the time. I didn't want him to die. I was able to give him a mixture of some herbs and milk I got from an old lady, and that helped.

In Kibuye, I met a woman I knew from the market where we both used to work, and we hatched a plan to escape. Since the Interahamwe militia were still killing Tutsi, we decided to leave Kibuye at night. Over two days, we marched all the way to Gitarama, where we met R PF soldiers on July 20, 1994. They took us to Kigali in their car.

Back in Kigali, I met a female friend who let me stay at her house. My baby was still very sick, and I gave him milk and bathed him. Like other survivors, I tried to locate any remaining relatives and went to the Red Cross to see if they knew anything about the whereabouts of my family. I looked at the pictures of people who were still alive, but I couldn't find any of my relatives among them. My previous house was now occupied by Hutu. Since I'd been renting that house before the genocide, I couldn't kick them out.

It was complete chaos after the genocide, with everybody taking what he or she could get. A Tutsi friend had taken my furniture and given it to his sister. She refused to return it to me. When I reported this to the police, a soldier went to the house of my friend's sister to investigate. She claimed I had lied about it, so I was not able to get the furniture back. I finally managed to rent a house in Kigali and I worked several jobs in order to earn a living.

Almost all of my family and in-laws had died during the genocide. Whenever I got sick, I had no one to support me. My father had escaped to Byumba, where the R PF were already in control. He died in 1994, though, soon after the genocide. Perhaps his death was caused by the beatings he had endured. I never got to see him again. I have only seen my mother once since the genocide.

In 1995, I married a cousin of my husband. We had three children together. I found out in 2005 that I am H I V positive. My youngest child was permanently ill, and we went to the hospital to test him for HIV. When he turned out to be HIV positive, I also got tested. I think I was infected with HIV during the many rapes I had to endure during the genocide. When I found out that I was HIV positive, I had my other children tested. The child I had had before the genocide turned out to be infected with HIV as well, probably because I had to breastfeed him after I was infected. In November 2005, my second husband got sick, and he died only three days later. He had asthma and was HIV positive, but at that time we didn't know he was also infected. I think I might have been the one who infected him.

I have managed to find jobs here and there, but it is really hard, because I don't have a lot of education. Currently I am selling charcoal. The house we were building in my husband's birthplace was destroyed during the genocide. I now live in a house in Kigali that was given to me as a gift by some relatives who currently live in Belgium. I experience a lot of trauma all year long, especially during the annual mourning period for the genocide in April of each year. My stomach, my head and my private parts ache a lot. Sometimes my private parts start bleeding without a reason. I live in constant fear, wondering who will take care of my children if I die.

I think I have forgiven the man who killed my daughter and my in-laws. Maybe it is because he asked for forgiveness, and his request seemed to be heartfelt. He told me that my daughter and my in-laws were beaten with a nail-studded club then thrown in a ditch, where they spent two days in agony. Their bodies were covered with soil and later thrown in another ditch. The man who killed my first husband fled right after the genocide and is no longer in Rwanda. I don't know where he is now. I don't go to the *gacaca* courts anymore, because the people we are accusing are being released. I don't see the point in taking the risk of sharing my testimony there if it doesn't make any difference.

My life is hard. My children go to school, and I need to pay for their school fees and materials. I would like to get some support for them without being a beggar. One day I would like to have my own business where I can sell clothes. I tried to set this up once before, but I didn't have enough money to do it.

I shared my testimony hoping that this book will spread my message farther than I could ever do myself. The international community should help us to rebuild our hopes and dreams.

ADELA MUKAMUSONERA

BORN: 1966 (date and month unknown)
BIRTHPLACE: Nyakivala, southern Uganda
(near the Rwandan border)

WANT TO SHARE my testimonial with you for two reasons: I want the world to know what happened here in Rwanda and what we had to endure, and I want to heal myself by unburdening my heart. When more people learn the truth, I hope that their voices will add to the chorus of those ensuring such crimes never happen again.

In 1959, before I was born, my family left Rwanda for Uganda because of the discrimination that Tutsi faced. I was born in Uganda, but my family returned to Rwanda when I was just a child, because my father worked with Catholic priests from Belgium who wished to start a congregation here.

Despite the hardships that Tutsi experienced, we made the most of our lives in Rwanda. My family lived in Kigali. In 1987, I went to school to learn to be a seamstress. The school was located near a FAR soldiers' training camp, and that is how I met my first love. He used to come from the camp to visit me at school, and I got pregnant soon after we met. He rented a house for me to live in when he was away fighting. In 1990, when my son was only one, my dear soldier was killed in a battle with the Inkotanyi in the north of Rwanda.

After his death, I moved in with my older sister, who was a tradeswoman. I survived by selling milk. That is how I met my boyfriend; he owned a truck and delivered potatoes from Ruhengeri, in the northwest of Rwanda, to Kigali. I saw him every day when he came to my shop to drink milk, and we soon fell in love. Five months after meeting my boyfriend, I moved in with him. He was so good to me and loved me very much. He also loved my first son as if he was his own. In 1993, I gave birth to my second son.

Despite my bond with my boyfriend, his family never accepted me or approved of our relationship, because I was Tutsi. I remember his sisters would always say that one day all Tutsi would die. Where we lived, Tutsi were a minority. Our neighbours put up with me, but only reluctantly. I always felt that, given the opportunity, some of my neighbours would harm or kill me. But all those thoughts were banished when I remembered that my boyfriend was a Hutu, too. I thought he would be able to protect me.

My boyfriend knew, even before the death of President Habyarimana, that mass killing would begin. I suspect he knew of the impending genocide because his family had very good relations with the Interahamwe. For that reason, shortly before the genocide began, my boyfriend took my sons and me to the Butamwa quarter of Kigali. The very strange thing was that he was doing this to protect us from his own family. I was only twenty-eight years old at the time. I moved back to my parents' old house on Mount Kigali, and my boyfriend returned to Ruhengeri. He thought it would be safer if we remained separate. That way we would draw less attention to our family.

My mother and my grandmother lived at my parents' old house. My father lived nearby with his girlfriend. My mother didn't own a radio, so we only realized that things had deteriorated when barricades sprang up on every street. On April 7, the Interahamwe militia started killing Tutsi families, looting their possessions and burning down their houses. We decided to stay inside because it seemed more dangerous to leave the house.

A few days later, while breastfeeding my younger son, I saw a group of Interahamwe militia armed with machetes, swords, spears, batons and other weapons approaching our house from across the street. I also noticed that a barricade had been erected in front of our house. I decided to secure my baby to my back and flee. I hid in a nearby bush, but my baby started to cry, which alerted the militia to our whereabouts. The militia soon found us. When they saw me hiding in the bush, the militia laughed loudly and shouted a phrase that I will never forget: *Akanyu karashobotse*, meaning "your last day has come." I was pushed to the ground and gang-raped by three of them right there and then. Once they were finished with me, they

Adela at home with her son and her mother

gave me a bag of corn and ordered me out of the neighbourhood they were in charge of. I immediately fled.

After what seemed like weeks of hiding in bushes with my baby son, eating nothing but the occasional cassava and sweet potato I was lucky enough to scavenge, I met my mother, grandmother and older son not far from our house. They had also been hiding. Their lives had been spared temporarily after they handed over all their property, including their house and their fields, to the Interahamwe. My mother informed me that most of my uncle's family had died after being beaten; their bodies had been thrown in a ditch. As we were talking, we heard people approaching. My mother and my grandmother decided to flee to our house, taking my sons with them. I decided to go to my uncle's house to see if there were any survivors among my uncle's family and perhaps to hide there.

On my way to my uncle's house, I was caught by another group of Interahamwe militia. They detained me, and the leader of the group, a twenty-one-year-old named Damascene, ordered me to strip my clothes off so that he could "see what Tutsi sex looked like." I recognized Damascene from before the genocide. He lived in a house in my neighbourhood. He was a quiet person, and no one really knew him. As I started to undress, he hit me on the head with a stone and hit my back with a club. He grew impatient with me and started to tear off my clothes himself. He pushed me into a ditch and raped me in front of his friends, who were standing nearby. Many other Hutu, who were my neighbours, were also watching. I knew them all. They watched and laughed, as if Damascene was an artist painting his masterpiece.

While Damascene raped me, one of the Interahamwe decided to call my father and force him to see what was happening to me. When my father came, he begged the Interahamwe to kill him instead of raping me, but they wouldn't. He ran back to his house, screaming in agony. When Damascene finished raping me, he offered me to the two youngest males in the group, who were young enough to be my children. They were both ordered to rape me. While they did, I felt like I was already dead. I was crying the whole time.

Damascene was responsible for one of the many barricades erected by the Interahamwe to prevent Tutsi from escaping. While he was busy raping me, some people took advantage of his absence and fled with their belongings. Eventually, Damascene noticed people running with their bags. He pursued them, leaving me in the ditch. After Damascene and his group left, a Hutu thug called Bajyahe, who had been watching, told me to run also, and he gave me his jacket. I covered my naked body with it and ran back home.

At home, I found my mother, my grandmother and my two sons. They had not been harmed, but they feared I was already dead. I would soon learn that after I was raped by Damascene and his thugs, another group of Interahamwe went to my father's house and beat him severely. The Interahamwe did not kill him right away. Instead, they gave him his date of execution. This was how the Interahamwe dealt with older Tutsi.

My mother, grandmother, two sons and I stayed inside our house for three days. Eventually we ran out of food, so I ventured into our fields to find something to eat. To my horror, I encountered Damascene there. When he saw me, he pushed me into a shallow hole, threw banana leaves on top of me and set the leaves on fire. I was being burned alive. I used my arm to shield my face from the fire, and I now have a long scar on my arm as a result. I think Damascene tried to burn me alive because he had no other weapons at hand.

While the banana leaves were burning, I heard people shouting that the Inkotanyi had taken over the country. It was a wonderful stroke of luck. Damascene heard this also and started running. That is how I escaped. I threw the banana leaves off me and climbed out of the hole. I returned to my house and waited inside with my mother, grandmother and two sons while the Inkotanyi and FAR soldiers fought outside. After two days, we made up our minds to leave; we heard many gunshots, and they seemed to be getting closer. Amidst the chaos outside, we didn't realize that the Inkotanyi had won and could have protected us if we'd stayed. Instead, we fled with others, including the Interahamwe, to the Congo. My grandmother stayed behind because she was too old to make the journey.

With my baby strapped to my back, I walked to the Congo with my older son and my mother. We walked every day. At sunset, we would go to sleep. It took us a week to reach our destination. In the Congo, we found shelter at a refugee camp. It was only once we were settled that we realized we were surrounded by Interahamwe who had escaped the Inkotanyi. Even so, we were too exhausted to make the journey back right away. I knew that

Tutsi girls were being raped at the refugee camp, but I generally felt safe. The Interahamwe didn't try to hurt us, since I was being "protected" by my former Hutu neighbours. My neighbours had killed people during the genocide, and I knew the only reason they were trying to protect me was to make themselves appear less guilty should I accuse them of their crimes at a later date.

After two months, my family decided to walk back to Rwanda. We didn't tell anyone at the camp we were leaving, for fear the Interahamwe would kill us. I knew they were afraid of Tutsi returning to Rwanda to accuse them of their crimes. My mother, my two sons and I made the journey back to Kigali together.

The Inkotanyi had control of the city. In Kigali we saw bones everywhere, but the bodies had already been buried. We returned to our old house to find that my grandmother was no longer there. My older sister, who had fled to the Congo with her Hutu husband, had returned alone and moved into that house. She told us my grandmother had passed away while we were in the Congo and the Inkotanyi had buried her body. For the first little while after our return, the Inkotanyi gave us food. When that food was gone, we started digging our fields again, and I farmed cassava, sweet potatoes, sorghum and beans.

Because of the rapes I endured, I suffered very serious trauma. My mother was also traumatized and she cried all the time. I started drinking, because I needed to forget about what the Interahamwe had done to me. I became an alcoholic and went mad, and was in and out of the psychiatric hospital. At the hospital, I was tested for HIV. That's how I found out I am HIV positive.

I continue to have problems in my private parts. I rarely have enough strength to eat and I have a permanent migraine. To this day, I am rejected by my Hutu neighbours, who all participated in the genocide. None of them come to my house, and they will not invite me to their houses. Only God has not rejected me.

I am alone in this world. My boyfriend was shot to death in June 1994 by the Interahamwe while he was transporting potatoes for Hutu in Kigali. It is strange to think that the Hutu continued their daily lives during that time as if nothing out of the ordinary was happening. My boyfriend was killed because of his relationship with me. I learned about his death after the genocide, when the man who killed him told me. I knew this man from before; we did not live far from each other. When he told me about my boyfriend's death, he acted as if someone else had done the killing and he had just been watching. Anyway, he is now in prison. My father died from the beatings he endured during the genocide. He died when I was still in the Congo, and my older sister told me the Inkotanyi soldiers had buried him too.

I don't have any extended family. Recently, I returned to Ruhengeri to visit my boyfriend's mother, but she refused to let me enter her house, saying that her son is dead and I should have died as well.

In 2007, I went to the *gacaca* courts to accuse Damascene of what he had done to me. He was convicted but released after less than one year. Considering what he did to me, one year is not enough. I think he should be in prison for his whole life. After his release, Damascene came to my house and demanded forgiveness. I think it's because he learned about unity and reconciliation when he was in jail. The government had already forgiven him by releasing him, he said, and now it was my turn to do the same. He asked me if I would forgive him in exchange for a cow. That really upset me. This man who reduced my life to nothing thinks he can make amends by giving me a cow? How can a human life be exchanged for a cow?

Damascene and his wife are now my neighbours. They are getting richer every day, while my situation remains the same. One time, Damascene passed by my house and saw that my mother was ill in bed. He gave her three hundred Rwandan francs and told her to go to the hospital. He put the money in my mother's hands, but she threw it back in his face. She did not want to take money from him. That is humiliation. It made me so angry! I might have forgiven him before, but I can't forgive a man who thinks forgiveness can be bought. Why should I forgive him? I don't want to be corrupted for forgiveness' sake. I can forgive, but not in exchange for money or a cow. I just want sincerity.

MARIE CLAIRE UWERA

BORN: August 16, 1970
BIRTHPLACE: Gacurabwenge, Gitarama

BEFORE THE GENOCIDE, I lived in Taba commune, Gitarama Prefecture, which is in central Rwanda. I felt at home there. In my free time I liked to sew. I lived with my husband and our two sons, not far from my parents and my seven brothers. My husband ran a bakery, and I was a tailor.

There were only three Tutsi families in our neighbourhood; the rest were Hutu. But we seemed to have a normal relationship with our neighbours. I knew that in 1973, when I was only three, some Hutu had burned our house and stoned my mother. This event followed Habyarimana's coup d'état, which overthrew the sitting president and resulted in many Tutsi being killed. When my father rushed my mother to the nearest hospital, the staff refused to treat the open wounds on her arm because she was a Tutsi, and my father had to heal her himself with traditional medicine.

My mother used to own a little shop in Taba commune, where she sold things like body lotion, soap and bread. On the morning of April 7, 1994, I stopped by her shop to buy something and saw that the surrounding shops were still closed. I asked my mother why the shops were closed, and she told me that our president had died the previous night. Upon hearing this, I felt very afraid, and I convinced my mother that we should return home together. My brothers were happy about the news; they said that if the president was dead, the time for peace had come. But my father did not share their opinion. He said that the time for the killing of Tutsi had come—and he was right.

Some days later, my mother and I ran into a rich man, one of our Hutu neighbours, who asked us where we were going. We were going to our shop, we said. He laughed out loud, then said, "*Akanyu karashobotse,*" meaning "your last day has come." We were very afraid. Not knowing what to do, we went to a nearby shop, where we sat down for a moment. Hutu who passed by asked us what we were doing there, and we told them we were afraid of the Interahamwe. They responded by saying that if we were scared of the militia now, we should wait until we actually met them. That frightened us even more.

In our area, the killings began on April 21, 1994. My father was a judge, and he was the first one to be killed. A group of Interahamwe came to our house and tried to destroy it with my father and brothers still inside. When my father went outside, they killed him immediately by striking him on the head with an iron pole. They left his body lying there. They covered it with eucalyptus leaves afterward, because it started to rot and stink. My father was the first Tutsi killed in our community because he was an intellectual and we were a wealthy family. Our neighbours thought we were cooperating with the Inkotanyi, and they were jealous that my brothers had gone to school, which was not usual in those days for Tutsi.

After the attack on my father the rest of our family—among them my husband, our two young sons, my mother and some of my brothers and nieces—fled. At the time, we were not sure who was trying to kill who, and we just followed other people. We finally arrived at a little nearby commercial centre, with shops selling manufactured goods, hoping that we could survive there. The *bourgmestre* of Taba, a man called Jean Paul Akayesu, came to the centre to ask us why we were there, and we told him that the Interahamwe were hunting us. Akayesu rejected us and told us to leave the place unless we wanted him to call the Interahamwe. Since we didn't know where else to go, we stayed. We were afraid, and had nothing to eat or drink except some coffee beans that we had found.

One day, some FAR soldiers arrived and took my husband to a police station. They beat him severely on his back. I would find out later that he was able to bribe one of the guards at the police station to let him go, but I didn't see him again until after the genocide. On another occasion, I remember a Tutsi girl of about fourteen who was taken from the commercial centre by an Interahamwe. I recognized him as one of my neighbours. The girl told us that she was raped by more than ten Interahamwe in one day. Every time she returned after being raped, they came looking for her in order to rape her again. After she returned from being raped a third time, there was blood streaming down her legs from her private parts. At this point she could not walk any longer, and she had to use her hands to drag herself. She cried a lot and did not say anything. As we were all waiting for death to come, we were not able to care for her, or anyone else, for that matter.

On Tuesday, May 3, 1994, the Interahamwe detained my mother and forced her to leave the commercial centre. I still remember this date so very well, since the nearby market was open, and the market only opened on Tuesdays. I decided to follow the Interahamwe with my two sons. We arrived at a big hole. There, my mother's clothes were ripped off and she was raped by Interahamwe who were not even twenty years old. Then one Interahamwe took a long sword and stuck it into my mother's belly. They also hit her with a club, and she fell in the hole. She was killed while she was still naked.

I did not feel anything except fear. My older son cried. I begged them to kill me, too. Though they beat me, they said they had no reason to kill me; they were not in a rush, since they could kill me anytime they wanted. Instead, they killed my older son, who was four years old, because, as a boy, he would have been able to fight them after growing up. He was thrown into the same hole as my mother. After the killing of my child, someone shouted that there were some cockroaches, and the Interahamwe left us. I sat there for hours and hours, not feeling anything. I wondered whether I was still a human being.

When I finally returned to the commercial centre with my surviving baby son, I saw that all Tutsi there had been killed. After three hours, I fled to a little forest nearby, where I hid with my son in a bush for about a week without food or water. My son cried a lot. I constantly hit him to stop him from crying and make him sleep again, so that we would not be discovered. But the Interahamwe found me with the aid of their dogs. One of them asked me if my child was a boy or a girl. I told him that my boy was a girl, and he said that he was going to make me his "wife" and that my "daughter" would replace me when I did not satisfy him. He took the two of us to his house, where he ordered me to cook some beef for him. I saw that the cows for the beef were from my house; someone else had slaughtered them and given them to the Interahamwe.

I knew this Interahamwe militiaman. He was called Yubu. Before the genocide, he had told me many times that he loved me, and I had always rejected him. Now it was his time to take revenge on me. He told me that he was going to do to me whatever he wanted. I never truly understood the meaning of those words until the day he inflicted his savage desires upon me. He abused me in every kind of position: from behind, in front and even with his fingers. The very first day he raped me, I begged him to kill me, but he said that I still had a lot to endure. I lived that hell on earth every day for about three weeks. Even though I was not locked in the house, I was afraid to go out, because other Interahamwe militia might kill or rape me. Yubu hardly spoke to me, and he did not want me to do any household chores, as he was afraid I would poison him. I stayed in the house doing nothing; I was too afraid to do anything.

One of my brothers somehow found out that I was there and came to see me. He told me how I could escape from that evil when Yubu was not around. But on his way back to his hiding place, an Interahamwe who was a former neighbour saw my brother and killed him instantly with a sword. I found out the next day that my brother had been killed, because I overheard people passing by the house who said so.

I felt so sullied and so dirty. Around June 16, 1994, which I remember because I was counting the days since my mother had died, I managed to escape with my son through a window at the back of the house. I didn't want to use the front door, in case people saw me and pursued me. I have a scar just above my eye that I got when I was fleeing Yubu's house. I finally decided to escape because I was afraid of being killed by Yubu, and what he did to me made me feel like I was being killed already.

I spent the night in a hole in the ground. The next day, I went to see a Hutu woman who was my friend. She refused to let me into her house, because I was a Tutsi and it would get her into trouble. But one of the woman's nieces saw me and took me to the outdoor toilets behind the woman's house, where I spent the night. The next morning, the woman's brother and

Marie Claire at the mass grave where her father
and other victims of the genocide are buried

his mates found me. They ordered me to get out of the toilet and threatened to call the Interahamwe if I didn't cooperate. So I went to a big sugar cane plantation near Nyabarongo River and hid there. While I was there, I ate sugar cane. My son was very hungry, and he had lost a lot of weight. I tried to feed him sugar cane by chewing it for him first.

After about a week of hiding there, a Hutu man with a gun found me. He took me to his house and raped me every day, sometimes four times a day, for about two weeks, until the RPF took over the country. I could not escape, since I did not have any other hiding place, and I could not refuse, because he would call the Interahamwe. During this period he made many cruel remarks. He would taunt me and ask me how I was going to survive with such a young child, and say that all my Tutsi "brothers" were dead. Like Yubu, this Hutu man did not want me to do any household chores, because he was afraid that I would poison him. I was hurting so very much. I asked God to let me die.

When the RPF arrived in that area on July 4, 1994, the Hutu man came to the house with a group of Interahamwe militia to kill me, but the RPF saved me by shooting them. The RPF came and took my son and me with them, gave us clothes and shoes and brought us to a safe place near the Nyabarongo River, where many survivors from neighbouring areas had assembled. There I reunited with my husband.

I never told my husband what had happened to me. I feared his reaction to the rapes, and I had no other relatives I could turn to. Even though he asked me a few times whether I had been raped, I always denied it. I lied to him and said that I was hurting because of the many beatings I had had to endure during the genocide.

We had three more children after the genocide. In 2000 I started feeling very ill, so I got tested for HIV and discovered that I am HIV positive. My son who survived the genocide with me was not infected, but two of the three children I bore afterwards also tested HIV positive. While my oldest son seems healthy, he has difficulties sleeping. Sometimes he falls out of his bed and starts running around. He does not perform well in school. I don't know why he's like this, but maybe it has to do with the gunshots he always heard during the genocide and the fact that I used to slap him in order to make him quiet. One of the most painful things for me is to see my children suffer for something they didn't do.

In 2002, my husband died as a result of the severe beatings he endured while imprisoned during the genocide. His passing left me in deep poverty. The house I lived in before the genocide was destroyed. I don't own my own house, and sometimes I don't have enough money for the rent. I don't have the ability to work, but I must feed and take care of my four children. I have psychological problems because my neighbours and my community don't know who I really am. Still, I don't mind if they find out when this testimonial is published. I want the world to know what really happened here in Rwanda in 1994. I would have died had I not received support from other survivors.

After the genocide I found my mother's body, with the sword still in her belly, in the hole where I last saw her. My son's body was also in that hole. I recognized his body because of the jacket he wore that day. Their bodies have now been reburied, as have the bodies of my father and my brothers who died during the genocide. The men who raped me are all dead. The ones who killed my family are being released, and I don't know what to do. The man who killed one of my brothers is still free, even though I accused him before the *gacaca*. He is a rich person; maybe that is why he is free. Living with the perpetrators of the genocide is a serious challenge for all of us who survived. Those atrocities must never happen again. Only God can bring us justice. I hope that God will also bring me hope for the future.

PASCASIE MUKASAKINDI

BORN: July 25, 1959

BIRTHPLACE: Karambo, Gikongoro

TO THIS DAY, when I think back to the genocide of 1994, a feeling of coldness comes over me and I start to shiver. I remember the freezing house where the Interahamwe enslaved me in nothing but my undergarments. But I still wish to share my testimonial with you to help let the world know what happened during the genocide and bring justice to those who suffered. I wish to have a better life. Without people who care about our plight, we will die.

My family has had a long history of suffering. My father used to tell me about the history of Tutsi oppression in Rwanda. In 1959, seven of my uncles and aunts were killed by Hutu, and their bodies were thrown in the Rukarara River, a large river in Gikongoro Prefecture. In 1963, some Hutu neighbours tried to kill my father, a Tutsi, but his Hutu father-in-law hid him on his banana plantation. In 1973, following the coup d'état by Habyarimana, we were forced to give a few cows to some Hutu neighbours so that they would not kill us.

In 1990, discrimination against Tutsi got much worse as news spread about former Tutsi refugees who wished to return to the country from Uganda. That year, I was living in Nyanza, in the south of Rwanda, with my husband and my child. Tutsi traders and teachers were killed, and others were jailed. Traders and teachers were among the first to be killed, since the traders were considered rich and the teachers were considered intellectual. Despite these killings, I wasn't afraid myself, since I felt there was no reason to kill me.

Before the genocide in 1994, I was a trader in second-hand clothes, and my husband was a truck driver transporting food all over the country. My husband and I came from the same area and we got married in 1984. We decided to live in Nyanza because my husband's job was there. Where we lived, Tutsi and Hutu shared everything. My mother was Hutu, but my grandmother was Tutsi. I was considered Tutsi since my father was Tutsi. Ethnicity didn't seem to matter to the ordinary Rwandan; it seemed to matter only to the people who wielded power.

A week before the genocide began, I was in Gikongoro, in southern Rwanda, visiting my parents. I saw Hutu forming groups here and there and buying strange weapons. On April 7, 1994, while I was still in Gikongoro, we heard that the president had died in a plane crash. Soon after, we heard Tutsi screaming as their houses were burned by Interahamwe militia on the orders of the prefect of Gikongoro and the police. On April 12, 1994, the prefect asked the policemen of that area why they had not yet started to "work" when in other places the police and militia had already finished. As soon as I heard this, I went to a man called Marcel, who was a friend of my parents. My father had given him a cow, which is a sign of great friendship in Rwanda. Marcel was a Hutu and a demobilized FAR soldier, and his wife was a Tutsi, so I went to see if he would hide me. He agreed, and I stayed in their home for two weeks, until the day the Interahamwe came to burn Marcel's house because all his in-laws had sought protection with him. During those two weeks I felt very frightened. I stayed in a room with all of the in-laws, and we couldn't do anything. I was waiting for death to come. I didn't know what was happening with my husband and our four-year-old child, who were still in Nyanza.

While the Interahamwe were placing dry tree branches around Marcel's house in order to burn it, Marcel told us to run out the back door. Some of his in-laws were killed during our escape. While fleeing, I encountered a group of about fifty Interahamwe militia. They detained me near the bushes next to the Gasebeya River and stole everything I had: my bag, my shoes and my watch. I also had a bottle full of milk, and they threw that milk on me, saying that Tutsi were like cats because we all liked milk. A few men tore my dress off, and one Interahamwe, named Charles, told me that he wanted to kill me so I could be the hundredth person on his death toll. I was paralyzed with fear. I was so scared I could not think, and I saw death right in front of my eyes.

That group of Interahamwe took me to some bushes to kill me. Just as they were about to do so, a man approached and proposed to buy me from them. I think he wanted to rescue me. He offered them twenty bottles of beer and two hundred Rwandan francs, but the Interahamwe said if the man wanted to make me his wife, they would first have to rape me. In the end, they refused to sell me, and they pushed me to the ground, injuring my chest. Afterward, the men raped me, one by one. Even the youngest ones in the group raped me, and they looked like they were no older than thirteen. Almost fifty men raped me in one day. I was too numb to feel anything. I had been abandoned by the Rwandan authorities who were supposed to protect me. After they were done raping me, they shoved a nailed club into my vagina, threw me into a thorny bush and left me in that state. I removed the club very slowly and dragged myself to a nearby river, because I thought the water from the river would help heal me. There, I slept. By this time I thought that my family must have been killed already, and I was waiting for death to come to me also.

After I awoke, I slowly dragged myself to a bush, where I hid for three days. Then I went to the home of an old friend of our family, a Hutu named Charlotte, who gave me a piece of cloth before ordering me to leave her house. She was afraid for her own security, because I was a Tutsi. My family was on a list of Tutsi to be killed as a priority, because we were considered RPF spies. This frightened Charlotte even more. From there, I went to a mountain called Nshyundo, where many Tutsi had found refuge in bushes. I stayed there for a week, until the Interahamwe came and burned the whole mountain. Many Tutsi perished in that fire, including my aunts and five of my cousins.

I escaped down the burning mountain to the Mwogo River. Crossing it would lead me back to my home in Nyanza. Before the bridge that spanned the river were two roadblocks, though, and around one hundred Interahamwe and FAR soldiers. They were staying in that area in houses that had belonged to a moderate Hutu, Minister of Agriculture Frederic Nzamurambaho, who had been killed earlier in the genocide. The Interahamwe spotted and captured me. They placed some banana leaves on the ground and ordered me to lie down. Before raping me, they ordered me to perform all kinds of gymnastics, including handstands, which was difficult because I was very weak. They tortured me in so many cruel ways, forcing me to take their penises in my mouth and shoving their penises up my nose. Their sperm fell from my nose onto my body and into my mouth. I wanted to vomit. I felt so stupid, and I could do nothing. They insulted and humiliated me. They told me that I was ugly and dirty and that I stank. No one was there to help me. After they finished, they took me to one of the abandoned houses they were camped in. I could not escape, because they would lock all the doors when they left to do their "work." I was the only woman in the house, and for two weeks many Interahamwe raped me every day, using me as their personal sex slave.

During those two weeks I wanted to die. Instead, I remained in that situation. I was wearing only some ragged underwear. I was really dirty and smelled awful. Since I was there during the cold season, I was always extremely cold. Talking about it makes me shiver all over again.

After two weeks, the Interahamwe heard that the RPF were getting closer. They beat me with nailed clubs until one of them said that I was dead and told his peers to leave me there. The RPF arrived a few hours later and took me to an RPF camp in Nyanza. There, they gave me all kinds of treatment. First they washed my entire body, which was very dirty. Then they treated my private parts, which felt destroyed. They gave me food and medicine, including penicillin. Slowly, I started to recover.

The Interahamwe militia and FAR soldiers who raped me did not think that I was a human being. My parents, my brothers and my sisters were killed during the genocide, and I don't know what happened to my husband and my only child. I don't know how any of my loved ones died, because we all fled in different directions, and the perpetrators have not admitted how my family members were killed. There has been a resurgence of genocidal ideology in Gikongoro, so people are reluctant to admit the crimes they committed.

I hate all men, and I do not want to hear about them. I feel the Interahamwe militia and FAR soldiers killed what I would have become. I am HIV positive. I am not able to work, because I am very weak and constantly ill. I suffer from headaches, chest aches, backaches and pains in my vagina, and

I have sinus problems as a result of the men who raped me in my nose. I live alone and have no one to help me, but I am surviving with the help of different organizations, which provide material and spiritual support. I find comfort and love through the support of those organizations and from seeing other widows who have the same problems. It helps me feel less lonely.

Some of the Interahamwe militiamen who raped me were imprisoned, but they are now being released. This is not justice. *Gacaca* courts were supposed to bring justice and reconciliation, but they are bringing more tears than smiles. The men who killed me should be better trained on how to treat survivors after they return to society. Soon, I will accuse some of the perpetrators myself in *gacaca* court. I am afraid of testifying against them, but I will not allow my fear to get in the way. Despite all that has happened to me, I can forgive those who ask for forgiveness from the bottom of their hearts.

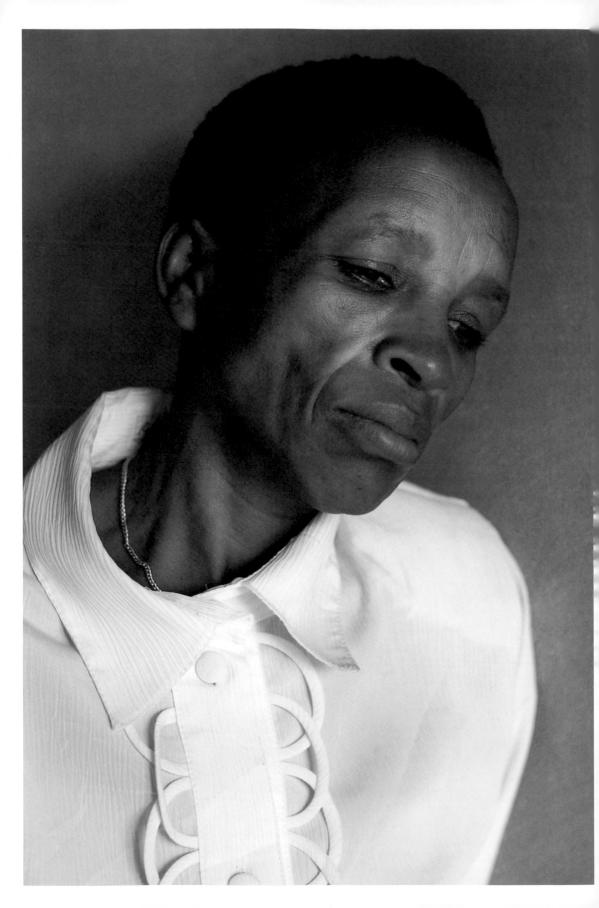

MARIE MUKABATSINDA

BORN: October 22, 1956
BIRTHPLACE: Ruhashya, southern Rwanda

BEFORE THE GENOCIDE started I had never experienced the discrimination or difficulties the Tutsi did. When I was in school, Tutsi children were forced to stand up and identify themselves so that the Hutu children could beat them up after class. Many Tutsi were forced to flee the country because of discrimination. But I did well in school. After my studies, I found a good job as a typist in the office of the *bourgmestre*. Not long after I started working there, I met my husband. His sister had married a friend of mine, and we met at her house. My husband was an animal caretaker for the ISAR, a government institute of agricultural research, and he was from Mugusa, another commune in Butare Prefecture. I quit my job at the office so we could live together in Mugusa. We were very happy together and had four children. When the genocide began, I was pregnant with my fifth child.

In the middle of April, I heard that Tutsi from neighbouring areas were fleeing the country for Burundi. The killings had not started yet in Butare, but shortly afterwards, President Sindikubwabo, the new president, came to Butare himself to ask the Hutu of Butare what they were waiting for and tell them to start their "work." The Hutu president didn't need to repeat himself, because local Hutu immediately took all the weapons they could find and started hunting Tutsi. Even though I was Hutu, I was in the same situation as Tutsi because my husband was Tutsi. Our house was torched by the Interahamwe just as other Tutsi houses were.

The local authorities ordered us to go to the ISAR, where my husband worked, in order to "protect" us. In hindsight, I can see they really wanted to kill us without spending time searching for us in our homes. Everyone, Tutsi and Hutu, was ordered to go. But as we made the journey there, someone stationed on a hill near the ISAR shouted for Hutu to return home, because only Tutsi were wanted at the ISAR. When we arrived at the institute, I lost sight of the rest of my family, except for the little boy I was carrying in my arms. Because there were so many people there, my husband and my three other children disappeared from my sight.

Some hours later, many Interahamwe came to the ISAR and started killing Tutsi. I saw babies crying for their mothers who were already dead, and women who were bleeding to death and asking for water to drink. I heard very traumatizing screams, and I could not stay any longer waiting for my hour to come. I ran, with my baby in my arms, and hid in some bushes in the ISAR compound. I stayed in those bushes for two days, but on the third, my son started crying from hunger. An Interahamwe found us, slapped my son and beat me on the shoulder with a nailed club. I fell to the ground, and the man left me, probably because he thought I was dead. Because I was hiding, people assumed I was Tutsi. A little while later, a man who used to work with my husband passed by, and I asked him for some milk. He laughed at me and told me that there was no milk left in the country.

After those three days of hiding from the Interahamwe, I left the ISAR during the dark of night. I spent the next two weeks in Mugusa, begging for food at the houses of people I knew. They wouldn't let me spend the night in their homes. I slept in the bushes, and during the day I begged for food for my baby. I felt that the rest of my family was probably already dead. When I had the opportunity, I would check among the bodies lying in the streets to see if I could find them.

One month later, the local authorities announced that the killing was over and anyone who was still hiding should return to normal life. Many Tutsi and a few Hutu emerged from bushes and from among the corpses. At the time, we didn't realize that genocide had occurred. We thought that the killings of 1959 or 1973 had merely repeated themselves, but not that these killings were meant to wipe out an entire race. In fact, the "normal life" the authorities were talking about was a return to the ISAR, where they could attempt again to kill us easily, by surprise.

At the ISAR, Interahamwe and FAR soldiers killed the remaining Tutsi men and raped all the women and girls. They worked as a team: the FAR soldiers would shoot Tutsi, and those who weren't dead would be finished off with machetes by the Interahamwe. They did this in front of everyone. I fled with my baby boy, and I was lucky not to be shot. I managed to run from the ISAR to the house of my sister-in-law, who was married to a Hutu. She was happy to see me, but she could only hide me for one week, because her husband was worried about having a Tutsi baby in his house. After I left their house, I wandered from bush to bush, feeding my son and myself with wild fruit. But I could not evade the Interahamwe.

The first Interahamwe I encountered approached me with a spear and told me he could either rape me or kill me. He raped me. Afterward he left me there. I went to another bush nearby, where I spent a week. While hiding there, I encountered another Interahamwe. He asked me how I was doing and then asked whether I could point to other bushes where Tutsi were hiding. I refused and said I was the only one hiding there. He replied that he didn't have time to negotiate with me, that I should just let him sleep with me. He said that if I refused, he would call other Interahamwe to kill me. He raped me, as well.

Two days after the second rape, I met another Interahamwe. I begged him to show me the way to Ruhashya, where I was born. I thought perhaps the Interahamwe there wouldn't kill me, since they knew I was Hutu. That Interahamwe said he would show me the way to Ruhashya only after raping me. After he raped me, he walked part of the way to Ruhashya with me. I didn't tell any of the men who raped me that I was Hutu, because I didn't think they would believe me. I was four months pregnant by that time, but they didn't care. My two-year-old son saw all that happened to his mother. Fortunately, none of the Interahamwe tried to hurt my son.

I arrived in Ruhashya after walking all night long carrying my little boy. My parents' old house had been destroyed, so I moved from relative to relative. My relatives stayed safe during the genocide because they were Hutu. They would welcome my son and me into their houses, but after a few days they would be afraid of the consequences of sheltering Tutsi and would tell me to go elsewhere. In Ruhashya, I discovered that my fourteen-year-old son had also survived. He had fled from the ISAR to Ruhashya to try to find me.

At the beginning of July, the Inkotanyi came and took us to Save, a sector in Butare. There, they had established a camp for survivors. The Inkotanyi fed us properly and clothed us. I stayed in this camp for a month. After that, I occupied the houses of people who had fled the country, moving from house to house with my two sons. Eventually, I returned to Mugusa. Because my house had been destroyed, I lived in the house of a neighbour who was an Interahamwe and had fled the country. That way, I could continue to take care of my fields. In September 1994, I gave birth to my youngest son. The government eventually built houses for survivors in Mugusa, not far from where I used to live, so I left the house of the Interahamwe.

After the genocide, I was always sick and was losing weight, so I decided to be tested for HIV. I found out that I was HIV positive. That was not at all a surprise after the rapes I had suffered. I believe my husband and my two other children were killed in the ISAR, though I have never seen their bodies. Now I live with my youngest child. My oldest child lives in Gisenyi with his cousin, and he is learning to drive. My second child lives at boarding school. I have felt increasingly weak in recent years, and I don't know how I manage to live. When I work in my fields, I only work for an hour at most, but I have managed to survive on what I farm.

I want you to know that the horrors people inflicted during the genocide are more than any human being can endure. For a long time after, I despised myself for what had happened to me. I hated everything that surrounded me, because it reminded me of what I had lost. I used to think that I would rather be dead than living with HIV, but I have received comfort from a charity that also provides me with antiretroviral treatment and food. I know now that I can continue to live with HIV. Sometimes I even forget that I am HIV positive. I no longer hate who I am, and I feel my love for myself grow.

IMMACULÉE MAKUMI

BORN: 1949 (date and month unknown)
BIRTHPLACE: Kibirira, Gisenyi

I AM GRATEFUL TO be able to share my story, because it releases a huge weight from my heart.

Life is hard. I have lived in dreadful conditions since the end of the genocide. My son died during the genocide, and I have no one else to take care of me. In 2003, I took an HIV test because I was experiencing physical problems. That year there was an increase in the number of people who discovered they were HIV positive; they had been infected during the genocide and were beginning to experience the physical symptoms of AIDS. I am HIV positive because of the rapes I survived. I also suffer from asthma and have serious problems with my stomach. I take antiretroviral medication, but it is not easy, because I need to eat nutritious food that I can't afford to buy. I am not accepted in my community, because no one understands how an old woman like me got infected with HIV. I don't know why people are so cruel to me.

My father had two wives, which was quite common in the area we lived in. My own mother had two children, my brother and me, and my stepmother had three children, two boys and a girl. From the time I was born, we lived in Kibirira sector in Gisenyi, in the northwest of the country. Hutu and Tutsi there generally got along well with one another, though the Tutsi were richer. Naturally, Hutu were not happy with that, and they often stole

Tutsi possessions. In 1959, when I was ten, our Hutu neighbours set our house on fire. My parents decided to keep me safe by taking me to my older stepsister's home. She had married a Hutu, and she and her husband hid me on their banana plantation.

My husband was a Hutu and also from Gisenyi. We had been distant neighbours, and our parents were friends. In fact, our grandmothers were sisters, so technically we were second cousins. We met in 1966 and got married a year later. We moved to Kigali because my husband found a job there. For me, there was little difference between our old home and our new home, because Hutu were far in the majority in both communities. I had some friends and relatives in Kigali, though. My husband's family rejected our marriage because I was Tutsi, but my family accepted it, especially since my husband's family had given my family an impressive marriage gift, which included beer and farming materials. The marriage gift is a Rwandan tradition, and is paid by the husband's family whether or not they approve of the marriage.

In the first five years of our marriage I gave birth to three daughters. It was really difficult to survive. We were very poor, because neither of us could get a good job. My husband had never gone to school, and I was forced to stop attending primary school after my parents' house was burned down in 1959. At first I had a small shop where I sold beer, and my husband worked at a company that produced digging materials to work the fields. My husband always told his co-workers to go to my shop to buy beer, but they would never pay me; they would pay my husband instead. I never saw any of that money, and I think my husband spent it on a Hutu woman he was having an affair with. Sometimes she came to our house, and I felt very sad that my daughters would see this. Because he spent all the money on this other woman, I was forced to close my shop.

In 1975, my husband ordered me to leave our house because I was Tutsi and his family had rejected him because of me. I decided to go to my parents' house in Gisenyi, and I was lucky to hitch a ride there with a truck driver. Because I thought I would have to walk all the way to Gisenyi, I had decided not to take my three children with me and had left them with their father. The day after I left the house, he brought home the Hutu woman. I was pregnant at that time with our fourth child, and, when I gave birth at my parents' house, my husband did not come to see his son.

Two years later, in 1977, my husband came to visit me. I didn't want to see him, but my mother pressured me to, as he was still my husband and perhaps wanted me back. Although we spent the night together, he left again the following day and went back to the Hutu woman. I was pregnant again, however, and later gave birth to our fifth child, a son. When that child was only three months old, he died.

There is a Rwandan tradition that a woman must go back to her husband if their child dies. So I went back to my husband, but, when I arrived at his house, I found out that he was in prison because he had stolen mattresses and furniture from the hotel where he worked. I begged the Hutu woman to let me have my daughters, but she refused, so I decided to return to Gisenyi.

In 1980, I gave birth to a sixth child, a daughter. She was not from my husband but from another man who had always liked me. We never married. I spent some months at his house, but I returned to my parents' house when I discovered that other people accused the man of being a thief. To punish him, some locals cut his leg off. We sometimes still meet in the streets and greet one another, but that's all.

In 1990, in retaliation for the RPF invasion from Uganda, our house in Gisenyi was set on fire by Hutu. My mother perished in that fire, and I had to live for two months in a church. In 1991, the UN World Food Programme built me a new house where the old one used to be, and I lived there with my children.

That same year, I was out walking with a young Hutu cousin of mine and some other Tutsi friends from Kigali. While my cousin was returning to his home afterwards, the police savagely beat and killed him. It was said that my cousin was killed because he was seen walking with a Tutsi woman. But the police accused me of the crime and also of being an Inkotanyi spy. They arrested me, threw me in jail and beat me the whole night. For the next week, I endured horrible conditions, living in a tiny room that was alternately a torture room, bedroom and bathroom. They would make me sit on the floor and would beat my legs and then stand on them. They also shaved my head and beat my head with the handle of a saw. Whenever they saw a dog, the police forced me to call it by my father's name.

I spent the next year in different prisons, moving from the police station in Gisenyi to the prison in Gisenyi and then to the prison in Ruhengeri.

Immaculée weaving one of the baskets she makes to generate income

I don't know why they made me change cells; maybe just to torture me, as I could hardly walk between places. I was imprisoned for a crime that I did not commit. Because of my imprisonment, my son had to stay with my brother in Kigali, and my daughter with friends in Gisenyi.

When I was finally released from the prison in Ruhengeri in 1992, I walked back to Gisenyi and stayed there for two days. But my house had been set on fire again; apparently some Hutu did not want me there anymore. I collected my daughter, and together we went to Kigali to pick up my son. My relatives in Kigali didn't really want to help me; instead, they gave me money and told me to look for a place of my own. That really saddened me. Luckily, I was able to find a place to live in Kigali. My children had to quit their studies, though, because we did not have any money for that. In 1993, my husband came to my house and told me he had left his wife for me. I got pregnant again, and we had another daughter in 1993. He never left his wife for me, however.

When the president's plane crashed in 1994, my son told me I should leave Kigali, and that is how I started my very long journey to survival. With my three children, I went first to my husband's house in Kigali. But his wife was not happy at all to see us, and she threatened him, saying that it was either her or my "bastards" and me who would live in that house. He initially agreed to take us in, but two weeks later told us to leave the house. I decided we should continue walking, without any specific destination, and we eventually arrived at a refugee camp in Gitarama. This was a camp of about two hundred people, set up by Tutsi. We stayed there for about three weeks.

One morning, as I was walking to the toilets in the refugee camp, two Hutu men abducted me. Those two men took me to a tiny forest nearby and ordered me to take my clothes off so that they could see what a Tutsi woman looked like. One of them raped me immediately in that forest, and while it was happening I could hear other people screaming and the sounds of guns going off all around us. The other man raped me after the first one was finished. After about an hour, I returned to the camp. My children asked me many questions about my long absence, and I assured them that I was all right. But I was terribly afraid and in a lot of pain. I didn't want to talk to anyone about what had happened. Instead, I found a certain comfort in being silent. I was afraid of all men and I still am, although to a lesser degree now.

In my absence, FAR soldiers had shot up the camp, and all the Tutsi had fled. Only my children were still waiting there for me. We decided to leave as well and walked to a camp nearby called Rushashi, near Gitarama, where about twenty Tutsi had gathered. Towards the end of the genocide, the Inkotanyi found us there and told us it was safe to return home. For the first three days, we stayed at the house of a Hutu woman who had also been at the camp, but then she told us to go home; she was afraid for our lives since her sons were Interahamwe. We left for Kigali.

Since the genocide, my oldest daughter has come to hate me. I was not there to take care of her during the genocide, and she cannot deal with the fact that her mother was raped. When I told her that I was HIV positive, she told me to kill myself so that I would not be a burden to her. My two youngest children even had to come to the hospital to protect me from my daughter.

I have forgiven the Interahamwe, because if I do not, I am the one who suffers. There is a curse on them, and one day they will pay for what they have done to me. My neighbours don't want me to testify at the *gacaca* courts, because most of the perpetrators will be leaving the prison any day now. I live in a neighbourhood with many *génocidaires* and I am afraid for my safety.

I have not received any kind of compensation since the genocide. I want the court to review my case of wrongful imprisonment, which I have shared with many people. The judiciary should review that case, but they still have not done so, and I don't know where to begin. I sometimes still meet my ex-husband in the streets, but we never talk. I could sue him for polygamy; he is legally still my husband, since we never divorced. I wouldn't be afraid for my life if I did decide to sue him. I want him to take care of our children. Some of them live in bad conditions, and I want my children to get their fair share of their inheritance when I die.

FAUSTIN KAYIHURA

BORN: August 1980 (day unknown)
BIRTHPLACE: Muyira sector, Butare

I DON'T KNOW OF any other men who experienced sexual violence during the genocide, but I know they wouldn't talk about it if they had. It was a very difficult experience, and not all men are brave enough to talk about it. It is considered shameful to be raped by a woman. I first spoke about it only in 2007. I don't want Hutu to hear about this, because I don't want to give them the satisfaction. They may ridicule me. I can only share this with other survivors of the genocide.

Before the genocide, we lived in Muyira commune in Butare. We were a happy family of eight—my parents, my four brothers, my sister and me. In 1994 I was only thirteen years old and the youngest of the family. I liked to play soccer. My parents were farmers. We owned cattle and a large expanse of agricultural land, where we grew beans, cassava and peanuts. Although we were not very rich, we were not poor. Our soil was very fertile, and we didn't need to think about buying food at the markets, because we had everything we wanted from our fields. We even had enough to sell at the market.

We had decent relations with our Hutu neighbours. We would invite them to our parties and ask them to help us when we needed it, and they would do the same. Nevertheless, numerous Tutsi had left school because the conditions were horrible. We were continually frustrated, and the teachers would sometimes make us stand so they could humiliate us before the

other students. The Hutu children would laugh at us and mock us. Being
Hutu seemed to give a person licence to be proud and to humiliate everyone
who was different, including Tutsi or Twa. There were few Tutsi in primary
school, and none in secondary school. We weren't given the opportunity.
Our ethnicity was written down in the school files. Because places in
schools were given to Hutu children, and Tutsi children were discouraged
from studying, many of us abandoned school. Only Hutu were encouraged

to go to school. Before the genocide, there were also some killings of the most intelligent Tutsi. I didn't know any of those people personally, but they were well-known Tutsi, such as teachers and important merchants.

By April 6, 1994, killings had already started in Kigali. We only heard about this on April 15, when many Tutsi who were fleeing and passing by our region told us. The genocide started later in our region, because the prefect was Tutsi, and he was able to delay the killings, until he was killed himself. I wasn't with my family at the time the genocide started, because I was watching over our grazing cows. When I returned to our house, I found it empty, and I decided to flee to a Tutsi friend of my father's, who lived near a Catholic church. From his house I could see that our house was on fire. I learned later that, while I was watching the cows, my family and other Tutsi from the region had fled to a commercial centre with shops not far from our house, where they spent two days in hiding. The *conseiller*, the head person of the sector, told my family to stay at the centre so that they would not be killed. He actually wanted them to stay so that they could be easily killed, all together. When the Presidential Guards came to Butare, my family overheard them asking the Interahamwe why the militia had not started their "work" yet. Soon after, the prefect was killed, and then killings started to happen in Butare.

I spent two days at the house of my father's friend. On the second day, when I saw two buses full of Interahamwe coming our way, I decided to leave. While running from the house, I heard people say that many Tutsi from our area, including my family, were still in the commercial centre. The people who told me that were fleeing from the commercial centre; the Interahamwe there had stolen their cows and chased these people away.

I decided to hide under some nearby bushes. Some Tutsi were killed close to me, but the Interahamwe did not see me. At night, as soon as the Interahamwe militia weren't looking, I would change my hiding place, hoping this would prevent them from finding me. After about a week, a Hutu woman found me and took me to her house.

The woman locked me in her house. I was only thirteen, and the horrors I experienced in her house were more than I could endure. She forced me to have sex with her. She raped me three times a day for three days. She made me lie on the floor, and because I did not have any experience with sex, she instructed me on how to do it. She would stroke my penis up and down with her hands first. Because I was still young, I had a hard penis fairly quickly, and then she would force my penis into her vagina. Sometimes she forced me to go on top of her, and sometimes she went on top of me. She was much stronger than I was, and since I was afraid, I did everything she told me to do. She also threatened me, saying that she would call the Interahamwe if I did not cooperate and that they would surely kill me. I don't know why she did this to a young boy like me, but she didn't have a husband, and it seemed she saw me as her husband. It was pure cruelty, especially considering my young age.

It seems unbelievable, but it is true. I don't have the words to describe what I was living in those days, but I know that I don't wish it for anyone else, not even my worst enemy. I cried and screamed the entire time. I felt empty. I did not feel anything: no pain, no fear, nothing. I don't recall her saying much to me, but my senses were no longer working. I remember hearing cries and people yelling outside. Somehow I was still alive, and I was thankful for that. During the evening of the fourth day, I told her I had to use the outdoor toilet, and found the courage to escape.

I didn't know where I was going. I only wanted to go far, far away, to someplace where I would never see that woman again. I hiked up a nearby mountain called Nyamure. As it turned out, my family and others from the commercial centre had been gathered there for some days, since the Interahamwe militia had attacked the commercial centre two days after my family arrived there. I was reunited with my family the day I arrived on the mountain, and we were very happy to see each other again. Because I had thought they were dead, it was a miracle to see my family alive again. We shared what had happened to us, but I didn't tell them about the rapes. They told me that after they left the commercial centre they went back home to bury an old woman. She was the first who had been killed in our region, and my family had heard others say she was hacked to death, so they wanted to give her a decent burial. However, some Interahamwe neighbours told them not to do so, because they wanted to feed her to the dogs. My family got frightened and fled to Nyamure mountain.

On the same day that my family and I were reunited, we were attacked by the Interahamwe. There were many Tutsi on the mountain—from Gikongoro, Nyanza, Butare and Gitarama—and to protect ourselves we threw stones at any Hutu who tried to climb up. Because of this, the Interahamwe

94

could not climb the mountain and fight us, but they shouted that although they hadn't been lucky this time, they would be the next time. I stayed three days on that mountain, and we survived three attacks from the Interahamwe each day. On a Sunday night, when it was raining, I fled with some Tutsi from Gikongoro who knew the way to Burundi. The decision to leave felt suicidal, because the mountain had been safe up until then. But the situation we were in was never good, so I decided to follow this large group of Tutsi. Because it was late at night and I couldn't make out who was who, I found out only the next morning that my second brother was in this group, too. The rest of my family had stayed on the mountain.

The day after I left with the others to escape to Burundi, the Interahamwe, with fresh support from the police and FAR soldiers, attacked the mountain. The Tutsi who remained behind were no longer able to fight them, as the attackers had brought guns and grenades. The Interahamwe killed whomever they could lay their hands on. Those who were not killed immediately, but were severely wounded and unable to move, were finished off later with machetes. My family and others died during this attack. After the genocide I found their remains still on the mountain.

With the group of people who knew the way to Burundi, I fled towards the Kanyaru River, which forms the border between Rwanda and Burundi. For almost our entire journey, we were followed by Interahamwe militia. At some point we ran into a roadblock manned by Interahamwe. In our panic, one part of the group ran in the direction of the main road, and the other towards the sorghum fields. Only the latter group, of which I was a part, survived. We ran for about six hours. Eventually, the Interahamwe abandoned their pursuit of us. After we reached the sorghum fields, we walked through rice fields in the water and long grass, so the Interahamwe's dogs were no longer able to track us.

When we arrived at the Kanyaru River, a Hutu man saw us. While pretending to help us find a boat to cross the river, he went looking for Interahamwe to kill us. Many of the Tutsi tried to get across the river by tying women's clothes together and forming a cord, but it was still very difficult to cross. There were many Tutsi corpses floating down the river, and that made it almost impossible to reach the other side.

Some people committed suicide by throwing themselves in the river the moment a group of Interahamwe arrived. They preferred to drown rather than be chopped to pieces by the Interahamwe. I didn't know how to swim either, but some of us were able to ask for help from some Burundian soldiers positioned on the other shore. The soldiers tied a cord around a tree on the Burundian side of the river, then crossed the river and tied the cord around a tree on the Rwandan side. I managed to save myself by holding onto this cord while crossing the river. I was so grateful to God for allowing me to make it across safely. My second brother survived in the same manner. Hundreds of Tutsi had left Nyamure mountain; only forty-seven of us survived.

The local authorities in Burundi took us to a Catholic church where about a thousand Rwandans had sought refuge. We stayed there for about a month and were given some food. At the end of that month, a white woman arrived with some big trucks. She wanted to take us to a camp called Bunyari, near the border with Tanzania. I think she wanted to kill us, though, because that camp was full of Interahamwe. We all refused, and she got very angry. She kept pressuring us to go with her. Instead, we left the church and went to the main camp in Burundi, called Kiyonza, which had been set up by Tutsi survivors. We stayed there for a week, until the end of the genocide in Rwanda in late June. After that the Inkotanyi arrived and helped take us back to Rwanda.

Before returning to my birthplace of Muyira, I stayed for over a month in a refugee camp in Bugesera, because Muyira was not yet under the control of the RPF. When I was finally able to walk back home, I met my former neighbours again. Some of them must have participated in the killings, but I wasn't afraid.

Of my eight family members, the only one who survived the genocide was the brother who had crossed the river with me. He did not join me in Bugesera after we left Burundi, but instead joined the RPF in Ruhengeri, because he wanted to do something good for his fellow Tutsi and his country. After all that had happened, he no longer felt safe and comfortable in his birthplace. After I returned, I learned that one of my other brothers had died on the first day of my family's stay at the commercial centre. Apparently he had gone back to our house to collect our cows, and a little while later, the wife of another one of my brothers and her two daughters saw him writhing on the ground. A militiaman pointed out the body to them, because he knew they were related. The militiaman killed my sister-in-law, but her two daughters managed to escape, and they were the ones who told me all this later.

After the genocide, I tried to continue my secondary school education. It was very difficult because I constantly saw visions of the woman who had raped me. I know she died, but I don't know how. In my fifth year of secondary school, I decided to stop going. I was living in a boarding school and felt very lonely. I was thinking more about our house and about how to cultivate the land to have something to eat. I am now cultivating the land, and I live in a house that I built all by myself.

I hated myself for a long time. I hated my life and wanted it to end. I am so thankful that I have now found people who care for me. They rescued me. They helped me to rebuild my house after the roof was destroyed by heavy rainfall. I also met women who showed an interest in me, who listened to me and wanted to know me. For some time, I hated all women and did not want to see them, but I am now healing. Now I have seen the other side of women and human beings in general, the good side that I had not known since 1994.

What I hear in *gacaca* court is unbearable, though. For example, in one of the trials, I heard that my aunt's arm was chopped off and that she was forced to eat it. After she did this, they killed her. Although I still testify, I find it harder and harder to do so. The perpetrators plead guilty and get released quickly, and they start killing again. Personally, I have not received any threats or intimidation. Not yet; it might just be a matter of time. Even though the government is pushing us to testify for unity and reconciliation purposes, it is very difficult for us, the survivors of the genocide.

I would like to study again, but I am afraid I may not be able to do so, since it has been such a long time since I was at school. I would also like to start my own business, maybe a shop where I could sell things like clothes, soap and body lotion. My house is still not strong enough and could fall apart any time heavy rain falls. I wish that someone could help me with this. I live all alone, which I find very difficult. Maybe someday I will get married, but I want to live in better conditions first.

FRANÇOISE MUKESHIMANA

BORN: 1968 (date and month unknown)
BIRTHPLACE: Bugesera

EVERY TIME the annual mourning period for the genocide approaches in April, I feel a terrible pain in my head and in my womb. I go to the toilet every five minutes, and I feel really horrible inside. When people counsel me, I feel the pain disappearing, little by little. I have been comforted by meeting new people, some of whom have become my sisters, brothers and children. Yet I do not feel like living in my community. I just want to live alone, on my own, and have nothing to do with other people—especially Hutu.

My family is originally from Gikongoro, in the south of Rwanda. My father told me that in 1959 my grandparents were forced by the colonial regime to move to Bugesera, just south of the capital, Kigali. The regime wanted to expel Tutsi from nicer areas like Gikongoro. In 1973, Hutu killed my grandparents. That was the year of the coup d'état, and many Tutsi were killed. My grandparents were not spared, because everyone in Bugesera knew they were Tutsi.

My mother died when I was still very young. My father was a farmer, and I grew up with six brothers and sisters. I spent my childhood helping my father farm, because he could not afford to continue sending me to school. He could only afford to send my older brother to university, because he was the cleverest of the children. The community I lived in was mixed, with mostly Tutsi and some Hutu. While Hutu were the minority, we got along easily with them, because quite a few Hutu men married Tutsi women.

That all changed in 1990. Between 1990 and 1992, the Interahamwe killed Tutsi boys from Bugesera after the boys were accused of hiding suspected RPF spies. Many of the boys didn't even know that the term cockroaches referred to people. Tutsi boys who were not killed were forced to flee the country in order to escape death. I remember that my older brother returned from university sometime in late 1993 and told our father that Hutu would soon be killing Tutsi. He said that the best thing to do was flee to Burundi until the crisis was over. My brother went to university in Butare, and his Tutsi classmates had joined the RPF, so he had a strong sense that something bad was about to happen.

My father wasn't sure how much of that was true, so he decided to stay in Bugesera. He just didn't believe mass killing would occur. Instead, we left our house periodically and hid in bushes close to our home. At the time, Tutsi houses were being burned by Hutu, and we didn't want to risk being burned in our own house. From June 1993 until the beginning of the genocide, we stayed in the bushes and returned to our house only to pick up food.

I remember that, when the genocide began in 1994, a bus full of FAR soldiers in uniform arrived in our neighbourhood, and one of the soldiers asked people why they had not started killing Tutsi and slaughtering our cows. No one said anything, so the bus continued on its way. Nearby, three young Tutsi men were walking along the street. When the bus got close to them, the boys ran, and a soldier ordered an Interahamwe to kill them. The Interahamwe ran after the boys and killed one of them with a machete. That boy was the first person to be killed in Bugesera during the genocide, and many more followed his fate.

One of the first things the Interahamwe militia did during the genocide was to remove all the boats from the Akanyaru River, which led to Burundi, preventing any means for escape. After the death of that young man, our family started to hide in bushes that were farther from our house. The Interahamwe were hunting Tutsi with dogs by then, and they found our hiding place in the bushes three days later. That is when they killed my brother-in-law and five of my brothers and sisters. I don't know how they were killed, but when I fled from the bushes where I was hiding, I saw their bodies lying on the street.

My remaining brother, my father and I managed to escape, and we went to the home of a Hutu man in Bugesera to whom my father had given a cow. The man showed us to a hiding place outside his house, on his banana plantation. But the next day he told the Interahamwe where we were hiding, so they came and captured us. They forced us to go to their favourite bar in Bugesera, all the while saying it no longer mattered that our father had given most of them cows, because we were Tutsi snakes.

They ordered my brother to dig his own grave outside the bar. When he was in the middle of doing that, they ordered him to lie down in the grave to see if it would fit him. My father couldn't bear to see what was happening, and he begged to be killed by the Interahamwe or to be let go. They let him go.

My father went to a roadblock and asked the Interahamwe there to kill him. The Interahamwe said he was a snake, and with their machetes they cut him on the neck and legs. My father, who was a tall man, was forced to go down on his knees. That was the Interahamwe's way of cutting him down. My father died at that roadblock. We could see all of this, because the roadblock was not far from where we were.

Back at the grave, the Interahamwe hit my brother with a huge club and told him to look at his sister for the last time. As he looked at me, he begged them to kill me first, because he feared that I would die of pain. Instead, they continued to bash him, until he died looking into my eyes.

The Interahamwe then proceeded to discuss how they would kill me. One of them argued that it would be a great mistake if they killed me without humiliating me first. He said that they should strip me naked and do to me all that they wanted, in order to tell others that they had been thorough in carrying out their "work." I was nothing but an instrument of gratification for them. The men ordered me to undress, and I could do nothing but obey. After that, they asked me if I still refused to have sex with them. Tears burned my eyes, and I started weeping. They laughed at me, saying that there was no one left to hear my cries and no one to stand with me. They ordered me to lie down, and a man I had refused to date before the genocide raped me first. Before he raped me, he said I now had no choice but to accept him. After he was finished, another raped me, and another and another, until I did not have the courage to keep count.

These men were so sadistic that they tried to cut my vagina into two parts with a sword in order to share me. I still have the deep scars on my pelvis today. I was bleeding so profusely that the next man about to rape me did not do it, saying that I was disgusting. All of this happened during the daytime, in front of the bar. Many Interahamwe were watching, dancing and laughing at me. The whole time, I felt nothing. I thought I was going to die. An old man passed by when they were about to kill me and quoted a Rwandan saying: "If you drink of a cow's milk, you cannot kill it." He added that if they killed me after raping me, my blood would always remain on their hands. Rather, they should leave me there and let me die by other hands.

Despite my wound, I managed to put some of my clothes back on and flee to the area under a bridge not too far away. I stayed there because it was a good hiding place. I knew that some traditional herbs growing among the bushes would help my wound to heal, so I left my spot under the bridge every night to find herbs to rub onto my wound. I ate nothing the entire time. Because I ate and drank nothing, whenever I went to sleep I thought I would not wake up again. I was always surprised when my eyes opened.

After three weeks, I heard some people walking on the bridge say that the RPF had rescued them. I decided to walk out into the light of the day, something that I had almost forgotten about doing. I saw two children on the bridge, and they saw me. They were frightened by my appearance and started to run away, but I gestured to them and they came back. They helped take me to a camp that the RPF had established. When I met the RPF in the camp, I was not recognizable. I was very dirty, with blood all over my body and my clothing in rags.

The RPF took all survivors to a camp called Kamabuye in Bugesera, about a twenty-minute walk away. There I met an older Hutu man whose Tutsi wife had been killed during the genocide. We stayed in the camp for three months. I left the camp with that man, and we went to Muyira commune in Butare. He proposed to me there. I agreed to marry him, but the marriage was not a happy one because his children, who were my age, still lived with him and they hated me.

When I first got pregnant and found out that I was HIV positive, I told my husband what had happened to me during the genocide. He comforted me and was supportive throughout the pregnancy. If not for the fact that I didn't get along with his children, I would have stayed with him. But they used to tell me I didn't have any right to live in their mother's house. After twelve years of marriage, his children continued to drive me crazy, so I left my husband after the birth of our third child.

My two oldest children were not infected with HIV. I'm not sure about the youngest, because he has not been tested. I live with all three of my children, and my ex-husband and I are still on good terms. Even now, he comes to see me and comfort me.

When I first separated from my husband, I didn't have a place to live. A Hutu man offered me accommodation in a room outside his house, in exchange for my help in cultivating his land. I cultivate for him once a week. I don't like this man, and the fact that he is a Hutu doesn't make it any better. But I must work for him, because I need a place to live. The farm work has been really challenging because of my HIV status. I am constantly ill and weak. Cultivating is really hard. If I want to survive, though, I must ignore my condition and work. Fortunately, since I started taking my antiretroviral medication, my health is improving.

I have not forgiven the Interahamwe. Those who wronged me did not face justice, and I cannot go to the *gacaca* courts as long as they are still free, because I am afraid the Interahamwe will kill me. Those who have been in prison since the genocide are being released and are shopping at the same market as we do. They should be sent back to prison and stay there for the rest of their lives or, better, be killed as they killed our people.

Knowing that there is someone who cares enough to listen to my experiences really comforts me. Now that I am talking about my experience with other survivors of the genocide, I know that I will feel better.

GLORIOSE MUSHIMIYIMANA

BORN: July 8, 1975
BIRTHPLACE: Gitarama

IT WOULD BE a lie if I said that I can forgive the Interahamwe.

I will never testify at the *gacaca* courts, because my sister was beaten on her way home from the *gacaca* court where she appeared as a witness. She had testified against our former neighbours and accused them of destroying our house and taking our possessions. Survivors of the genocide are living in terrible conditions, and those who make the mistake of testifying have been beaten or stoned. Even though we report the violence to the authorities, there is no change. The perpetrators should receive the punishment they deserve.

When I was growing up in Muhanga, Gitarama Prefecture, in central Rwanda, I lived in great harmony in a community full of Tutsi. We didn't have any Hutu neighbours. However, my primary school teacher was the *bourgmestre*'s wife and a Hutu. She was awfully cruel to Tutsi children. Nothing I could do would please her. She would beat us Tutsi without reason, call us snakes and ask us what Tutsi were doing among human beings. One day, she beat me until my dress was torn, just because I arrived at school a little late. I felt a lot of anger towards her and wanted to hit her back, but I also hated myself, because nothing I could do would make my teacher happy. In those days, I liked to sew clothes and do handicrafts.

In 1983, when I was eight years old, I had stomach problems caused by the poverty we were living in. My mother took me to the hospital at Kabgayi, about three hours away from our house. People there stared at my mother, whispering to each other that she must be King Musinga's granddaughter. My mother was very tall and beautiful, just like members of the king's family, but she was not related to him. Since she resembled the Tutsi king, though, others did not want to talk to us.

When I was growing up, my mother was always ill. Her legs were swollen, and she needed expensive medical treatment. Because my father couldn't afford my school fees in addition to my mother's treatment, I didn't have the chance to go to secondary school. That made me very sad, because I had always wanted to become a doctor or a teacher. My mother died in 1988. I was only thirteen.

A year later, I was surprised to hear that my father was going to marry a Hutu woman. It was so soon after my mother had died. This woman didn't love us, and she treated us badly. She gave my older sister, my older brother and me so many household chores to do that I was again prevented from going to school. After only one year, the woman left my father, taking all his possessions with her.

In 1990, a multi-party system was introduced in Rwanda. Many Hutu joined political parties and started stockpiling all kinds of weapons, especially machetes. Starting that year, we could not walk safely in the streets, and many of my friends also stopped going to school. In the bars and on the streets you could hear Hutu making speeches in which they proclaimed that the last hour of the Tutsi was very near. We were afraid that something bad was being planned. Back then, we had a Belgian priest named Michel, and, by the end of 1993, he was warning my father about a possible genocide. In the coming months, Hutu started burning houses and taking Tutsi possessions. In April 1994, we heard that the president had gone to Tanzania. There were whispers in the community that he had gone there to recruit more soldiers to help kill Tutsi in Rwanda.

Fearing for our lives, we fled our home on April 4. Our priest, Michel, drove my sister, my father and me to a stadium in Gitarama, near Kabgayi. Michel had planned only to rescue old women and children using his car, but my father happened to be nearby, so he took the last space in Michel's vehicle.

My brother walked to the stadium with my cousin. Along the way, the Interahamwe found them. They slit my brother's neck with machetes and beat him with a nailed club. My cousin fled to the stadium, and he told me later how my brother had been killed. Michel dropped us off at the stadium and drove away without realizing that the Interahamwe were actually killing people in there, even before the president's plane had crashed. They started killing the men first. They stabbed my father with knives and beat him with a nailed club. I witnessed the Interahamwe beat him on the head with the club and then leave him on the streets for the dogs and vultures to eat.

On the day the president died, April 6, we heard screams, babies crying and the Interahamwe shouting that they would kill all Tutsi, without sparing women, babies or the unborn. My older sister, my aunts, my cousins and I either hid in the toilets in the stadium or pretended to be dead by lying under corpses. Women and girls were being raped outside the stadium, including one of my aunts and three of my cousins. They were all killed afterwards. The Interahamwe would return to the stadium to brag about their crimes after committing them. None of my aunts survived their stay in the stadium in the end. I felt so afraid; my mind was no longer working.

Two days later, a new group of Interahamwe militia came to the stadium. They continued to separate the men from the women, so that the men could be killed and the women could be beaten. Some of the women died from the beatings, and others were severely wounded. I remember a little girl named Sandrine, who begged the Interahamwe to stop killing us. They responded by saying that the God who would have saved us was frightened and left the country when the president died.

I saw girls and women disappear day by day. We all knew that they were killed after being raped. We knew because the Interahamwe said they were looking for other women and girls to rape and kill. My sister and I were spared because we were still too young. After a few days, there were only girls and young women among us. One night a priest from Kabgayi came to the stadium and took my sister, my cousins, some other children and me to a classroom located in a priests' compound. There we hoped to be safe. The priest had friends among the Interahamwe, and he had bribed them with beer for our security. He went a second time, to collect the remaining children at the stadium, but that time his car was stopped, and he had to leave those children behind.

We were fed at the priests' compound, but there wasn't enough food for all of us. Four days after we arrived, the Interahamwe came to search the compound. The militia weren't singling out the priests; they were searching everybody's houses. They saw that some pieces of the ceiling were missing and they realized that young men were hiding there. The militia summoned the men to come down. When they did, the Interahamwe hacked off their legs and arms and then plunged swords into their chests. The priests had all fled and hidden by then, because their lives were at risk for protecting us.

Later that evening, the Interahamwe returned to pick up young girls to rape, even girls no more than thirteen years old, because they had killed all the older girls and women earlier that day. One Interahamwe approached me and asked me to choose between life and death. I couldn't answer him, so he tore my clothes off and ordered me to lie down. When I refused, one of the other militiamen hit me on the back with a nailed club. I fell and was bleeding heavily. This disgusted the Interahamwe who had wanted to rape me, so he left me there.

More Interahamwe returned to the compound the next day. After ripping our clothes to pieces, they took seven girls, including my older sister and me, to a small classroom in the compound. There were six of them, and they spent three hours raping us, without taking a break of even five minutes. After all six had finished raping us, they left, saying that their "work" was calling. We all lay where we were because we were so weak. I felt a lot of anger and wanted to die.

When the Interahamwe returned later that night, we were still in the classroom, lying down. They spent the rest of the night raping us, and from that day on, being raped by six different men a day became our routine. The Interahamwe hardly spoke to us, except when they ordered us to come to them in order to be raped. We had to go through these horrors for one week. We were too weak to escape that place; we could barely get up on our feet. Hunger killed several of the girls who were in that room. Only four of us survived.

Some soldiers came into the classroom on June 2. They didn't look like the Interahamwe we were used to seeing. They were very kind and gentle, and we eventually realized that they were the Inkotanyi. They brought us clothes to wear, because we were still naked, and fed us little by little. The Inkotanyi carried those of us who could not walk and took us to a Catholic church where local people were bringing water to the wounded. Sadly, five of the people who drank that water died immediately, because it was purposely contaminated by Hutu. The Inkotanyi moved us to Bugesera, where we remained until the end of the genocide.

I survived, as did my older sister, but the rest of my immediate family perished in the genocide. My sister and I returned together to Gitarama, but we found that nothing was left. We no longer had a house or a plantation. I went to Kigali to live with my surviving cousin, but it was difficult for me there, because he used to visit me at night and rape me. He threatened me whenever I was about to tell his wife about the abuse, so I chose to leave his home. I wandered all around Nyamirambo, a quarter in Kigali, spending the night under bridges or anywhere else. During that time, I would beg for food or do odd jobs, like washing clothes, for money. I hated myself. I felt worthless as a human being, since people just did whatever they wanted to do with me.

One day in 1999, I was sitting by the road when a stranger approached me. I had seen him walking the streets before. He asked me what I was doing on the streets, and he offered to let me spend the night at his house so that I could have at least one night of decent sleep. I accepted his offer, as I had no better opportunities. When we arrived at his house, though, he locked the door and said I had no alternative but to have sex with him. He raped me that night. The next day, telling him I had to use the outdoor toilet, I escaped.

I became pregnant from that rape, and I found an abandoned house in which to spend my days and nights. People feared me because they thought I was insane. I looked dirty, wore torn clothes and was living in an abandoned house surrounded by bushes. I didn't really care what they thought, since I felt I no longer needed human contact. Eventually I went to the hospital, where I gave birth to a boy named Mugisha in 2000. Someone I didn't know paid my hospital fees.

When Mugisha was born, I didn't like him at first. But I learned to love him. I haven't seen his father since he raped me. After Mugisha was born, a Tutsi man named Damien, a survivor whose leg had been cut off during the genocide, felt compassion for me and let me live in his outdoor kitchen. With him, I had a boy named Oscar in 2003.

I didn't love Damien, but I felt that unless I slept with him he would evict me from his kitchen. One day, when Damien was away, his sister came to the house and was very cruel to me. She didn't like the fact that I was living in Damien's kitchen and had had his child, so she started beating me. I left the place. Although Damien was not really interested in finding me, he tried to locate me because of his son. We are no longer in contact, but he still tries to support his son as well as he can. Because he is a survivor of the genocide, he is not a wealthy man.

I am HIV positive as a consequence of the rapes I endured during the genocide, or perhaps those I experienced after the genocide was over; I don't know. I am receiving treatment, and luckily my two children are HIV negative. The community in which I live has rejected me because I am HIV positive. They suspect the nature of my condition, because I am always sick and going to the hospital. I don't know where else to go. I can't expect any help from my neighbours, as I have no friends or relatives among them. I suffer from headaches and back pain as a result of what happened to me during the genocide. Since my parents died, I no longer feel happiness.

My church has provided me with some rent for the house I live in and school fees for my children. I hope that one day I may have a house of my own, where I could live with my surviving sister and another cousin. My sister lives with a friend now, and I am required to live in a house with friends, too, some of whom are also survivors of the genocide, because the church pays the rent for all of us.

I hope that my testimony will be proof of what happened in Rwanda. Some people deny this part of our history, but it is a reality they must face. I hope that some of those who read this testimony will help genocide survivors, because we urgently need help.

CLEMENTINE NYINAWUMUNTU

BORN: November 21, 1977
BIRTHPLACE: Rusatira, in the south of Rwanda

WHEN I REFLECT ON my lost childhood, I have a feeling of such extreme sadness. I lament whenever I remember all the dreams that I once cherished and that are now forever lost. I lament when I remember all those men who repeatedly raped me during the genocide, those same men who broke and destroyed me and every single aspect of my life. Those same men who killed me, slowly but very effectively.

I do not love the person that I am. I have not grown up to be the person I wanted to be. I know that now, and I can never be that woman.

It wasn't always like this. I used to live in a happy family with six children. My father worked in a manufacturing company, and while I could not say that we were rich, we were never poor. We shared everything with our neighbours, Tutsi and Hutu alike, and most of them were our friends. I was in high school, and it was a miracle to see a person like me, a Tutsi, attending school. My life was wonderful. I have so many happy memories of celebrations and good times that I had with my family and neighbours.

That all changed forever during the years preceding the genocide. The signs of what was to come were all there: our teachers began separating us, the Tutsi on one side and the Hutu on the other. The radio began calling us cockroaches. Neighbours who once were our friends no longer welcomed us.

During that time, many of us Tutsi knew in our hearts that one day we would die if things continued to progress the way they did. But we never knew that the day we feared was so close. Tutsi have always been a discriminated-against people in our history, especially since the so-called Rwandan revolution of 1959. There had been massive killings of Tutsi in 1959, 1963, 1973 and 1990. But none were as horrific as the killings that started in the capital, Kigali, on April 6, 1994.

Some weeks after the killings began, the president of that time, Sindikubwabo, visited Butare and told Hutu that it was their individual duty to kill every Tutsi in the region—to kill every Tutsi, irrespective of whether they were a family friend, a neighbour or even a spouse. The genocide went into full swing in our area, Rusatira, on April 20. I saw people fleeing their homes, trying to find refuge anywhere they could. But most were unsuccessful. After killing Tutsi, the Interahamwe threw their bodies in the river, saying that the Tutsi had to float back to their real home, meaning Ethiopia.

The government authorities and the Interahamwe ordered all Tutsi women to go to the ISAR compound, telling us we would be safe there because it was run by *bazungu*, white people. They told us no one would kill us in front of *bazungu*. But there were no *bazungu* there. It was the Interahamwe's strategy to gather us in one area so that they would not have to spend much time looking for us to rape.

We spent three days at the compound before the Interahamwe arrived. Once they entered the compound, they surrounded us very quickly so we didn't have time to react or run. They grabbed me, along with thirty of the most beautiful women and girls at the camp, and ordered us to leave the compound with them. When we arrived at the main road, we heard babies crying, women screaming and young and old men begging for their lives. The militia did not distinguish between rich or poor, important or less important. In their eyes we were all just Tutsi cockroaches. Tutsi who did not have the good fortune to die quickly from a bullet faced a much more agonizing death from a machete or spear.

I remember that, outside the gates of the ISAR centre, in a nearby forest, one of the Interahamwe said he wanted "to see what a Tutsi woman tastes like." Then the Interahamwe started raping us. Some Interahamwe held me down and took turns raping me, while others shouted insults at us, saying that we were nothing more than snakes and cockroaches. They

The path leading out of the ISAR compound in Butare

shouted, "Remember the past months when you were proud of yourselves and didn't look at us because you felt we were lower than you? Now that will never happen again." I felt that I was no longer a human being.

I lost consciousness during the time I was being raped by the fifth militia member. I woke up in the middle of the night, and the Interahamwe were gone. I was too weak to get up. An old Tutsi woman who was married to a Hutu found me and took me back to her house. Three days passed, and then she forced me to go to an Interahamwe member's house, because she thought we would both be killed if they found me at her house. She told me to accept his advances because it would mean I would not be killed. I was very afraid.

The Interahamwe man kept me confined as a sexual slave in his home and raped me repeatedly, sometimes three times a day, over the next week. One evening, I decided that I couldn't take it anymore. So I snuck out in the evening, when I knew the Interahamwe would be busy drinking and eating.

I returned to the old Tutsi woman's house, but I learned there that the Interahamwe who had enslaved me was very angry and had told her that if I didn't return, he would kill us both. I said to the old woman that even if she took me back to the militia member, I would escape again.

The old woman simply tossed me on the side of the main road. Before I even had a chance to catch my breath, another group of militia who were passing by overpowered me. They dragged me deep into the forest, where their leader raped me while the rest of them watched. He told me he had never before had the opportunity to have sex with Tutsi women, but now they had all become available. His friends told the man to kill me, but he replied that I was already on the brink of death and he would let other hands kill me.

I can't remember how long I stayed in that forest after they left. My eyes were open, but I was in a semi-conscious state. I could hear screams all around me. When I regained a little consciousness, I realized I was being pinned down by the pouring rain. I felt that I could no longer move my limbs because of what had happened to me. I stayed in that vegetative state in the cold rain for what must have been several hours.

Eventually an old lady passed by, and I heard her say to herself that I might still be breathing. I could hear everything she was saying, but I was paralyzed and could not respond. She kept asking me if I could hear her. Finally, I mustered up the strength to nod. Compassion filled her heart at that moment; she left for a few moments and returned with some food and water. I hadn't eaten anything for three days.

The old lady was too weak to carry me to her home, but she helped me to shelter under a bush and left me there. She visited me there daily, to see how I was feeling and to offer me comfort. She did all this without knowing me. She was always wandering in the bushes, looking for more people who were still alive. A week later, she took me to the home of a Hutu man who used to be a friend of my family's. His wife hid me behind their house, because she was afraid of her Interahamwe sons and what they would do to me.

The plan did not work. I was discovered by one of her sons, a priest. Despite his occupation, he informed me that I would have to accept his sexual advances whenever he was in the mood. If I wanted to stay alive, he said, I would not protest or utter even a word. One day, I could not take the rapes anymore, and I told the priest's mother what he was doing to me when she was away. She said to be patient and accept my predicament in order to survive; she also feared her sons. So I lived a hollow life and was raped every day I was there, for I don't know how long.

When the Inkotanyi arrived in the area, I was forced to flee with that family. They would have killed me otherwise, even though the Inkotanyi were my secret dream during that nightmare. The priest told me they didn't dare leave me behind, because I would accuse them of the things they had done. The priest's mother had developed an affection for me, and she treated me well on the journey from her home to a refugee camp in the Zone Turquoise in Gikongoro, in the south of Rwanda. The camp was full of Interahamwe. We stayed there for three or four days, but we left to return to their house after that. The Inkotanyi were approaching the camp, and the family said they would rather be killed by the Inkotanyi in their home than at the camp. Once we had returned to their home, the priest left one evening and never came back. In the morning his body was found outside the house, on the other side of the gate. We didn't know how he had died.

I am still haunted by the events of the genocide. It astounds me still that so few people showed me compassion during that dark valley of my life. What is most sad in my life is that I see the men who raped me walk freely in Rusatira. Only two of them spent time in prison, and they are now free like the others. I never went to the *gacaca* court when they were being tried, because I could not bear to see them again. I also could not tell the *gacaca* judges what I am telling you, because the rapists' supporters would have mocked and intimidated me. I didn't want to give them the satisfaction of seeing me traumatized again.

I am still traumatized by my experiences during the genocide fifteen years ago. I live day to day, and I do not have a tomorrow. I don't have a job. Because of the rapes I suffered, I am now HIV positive, and I am always ill. I have not continued with my studies; I had to drop out of school because my illness has made me desperate. I recently married, not because I am in love but because I felt lonely and needed a companion. I haven't told my husband about what I experienced during the genocide. I wake up in the mornings wondering why I continue to live. My neighbours used to always remark that I was going to die soon because of my condition. I ask you, is this a life worth living?

HYACINTHA NIRERE

BORN: August 1981 (day unknown)
BIRTHPLACE: Rusatira, near Butare

I WAS ONLY TWELVE years old when I was brutally raped during the genocide, at different times by different men. Because of the events that occurred in those months, I never got the chance to live my life as I had wished. So many of those dear to me were killed during the genocide. Only my mother, cousin, one brother and two sisters survived. I never had an opportunity to choose my destiny. I became a woman without even having a chance to be a girl. I did not know anything about sex; my parents never explained anything to me. I was not prepared to become a mother and take care of a baby. I have never loved my daughter, who was born out of rape, and even though I try my hardest to love her, there is still a long way for me to go. I often wonder why God planned this life for me.

When I meet the *génocidaires* on the streets, they do not seem happy to see me. Sometimes they do not allow my cattle to cross their fields. They do not say anything to me, and when I ask them about my families' possessions, they refuse to tell me anything.

I was born sixth in a family of nine children. Our female cousin also lived with us in Rusatira, in the south of Rwanda not far from Butare. We were all very happy and very close to our parents. Before the genocide, my mother was a housewife and my father was a policeman in Rusatira. My father got this job through an uncle who already worked as an accountant at the police station. My uncle was hired because he had good handwriting. Ultimately, the *bourgmestre* was not happy with having a Tutsi in an official institution and he told the inspector of police that my father was too old to be a policeman. The *bourgmestre* forced my father to quit his job in 1991. From that moment, my father was obliged to farm the fields in order to earn an income.

On another occasion, one of my brothers was jailed for three months for listening to Radio Muhabura, a station controlled by the RPF. Radio Muhabura promoted unity and reconciliation for all Rwandans—Hutu, Tutsi and Twa—and my brother secretly wished to join the RPF in Uganda. He was caught, together with three other young people, by the *conseiller* of the sector. They were listening to the radio in a sorghum field, where they thought nobody could see or hear them. I think the crime my brother committed was not listening to the radio, but being a Tutsi.

Even though we got along with our Hutu neighbours, we could sense, especially since the RPF invasion from Uganda in 1990, that there was no trust between us. For example, Hutu stopped their conversations whenever a Tutsi passed by. In schools, Hutu and Tutsi were made to identify themselves. The Hutu majority would then ridicule the Tutsi minority.

We didn't know what was happening in the rest of the country until April 14, 1994, the day the local authorities invited the Hutu, civilians and soldiers alike, to some special meetings. We knew these meetings were special since Hutu were screaming "Hutu power" and only Hutu were allowed to attend. Our Hutu neighbours told us our end was nearing.

The next day, we saw many trucks full of Hutu soldiers going to the neighbouring hill, which was almost exclusively inhabited by Tutsi. We were quite sure that these soldiers weren't going there to offer security; they went there to kill Tutsi. We also witnessed Tutsi from Gikongoro coming en masse to our area, and at that moment we saw the reality in front of our eyes. The genocide had started in Gikongoro on April 7, and now Tutsi were passing through Rusatira in order to reach Burundi to save their lives. Massacres were happening across the country, and Tutsi were definitely the ones who were being killed.

On April 15, my father left the house after our Hutu neighbour instructed him to go to a nearby roadblock to fight the invading RPF. The neighbour was following orders received from the *bourgmestre* and another high official of the sector during the special meeting the day before. These instructions were a lie told to kill Tutsi. Until then, no Tutsi had been killed

at a roadblock; my father was one of the first. On his way there, he met a group of Interahamwe militia, who abducted him and beat him to death with a nailed club near our house.

After my father was killed, some of our Hutu neighbours warned us to leave immediately if we did not want our lives to end in a few hours. We all took different paths. I followed my oldest sister, who was nineteen at the time. We met one of her Hutu classmates and another young Hutu on the road, and they said they would hide us in their house. Even though my sister's classmate was a Hutu, he had also been her friend for a long time; we trusted him. When we got there, it appeared that the house they were living in had been taken over from someone else. I later realized that they had killed the Tutsi owners and kept the house for themselves.

Whenever my sister and I wanted to leave the house and go somewhere, they refused, saying it was too dangerous for us to do so. One night, the young man came into my bedroom and ordered me to take off my clothes unless I wanted him to take me to the killers. I said I would rather die than do what he wanted. He replied that he didn't even know why he was arguing with me. He jumped on me, took off my clothes himself and raped me. My sister was living the same horrors in the next room with her classmate.

The young Hutu man raped me all night long, except when he was tired and took a break. I felt a lot of fear and thought I would be killed soon. After the first attack, the young man raped me again on the second day, twice. The two men went out killing Tutsi during the day and raped my sister and me during the night. We were forced to choose between being raped or killed, and they locked our room so we could not escape. There was nothing we could do in that room; we just felt so much fear. I was bleeding from my private parts and aching everywhere. I could not join my legs together, because it hurt too much.

After two days, while the two men were out killing, my sister and I managed to escape from the house. Since the house was near the street, we were able to ask passersby to tell the man who had married our aunt, a well-known Hutu, to come and rescue us. He did come and take us away from that house, and he and my aunt sheltered us in their home. We were there for a week. Unfortunately, the Interahamwe somehow found out that there were two cockroaches hiding in my aunt's home. We managed to escape before they arrived.

My sister and I went in different directions. On my way, I met a group of FAR soldiers. Some of them pointed at me, saying I was Tutsi, and one of them, named Emmanuel, asked me if I was. I said no, but he inspected my eyes, my ribs and the palms of my hands. Based on his inspection, he concluded I was a Tutsi and ordered me to follow him. I joined a group of five girls who were following the soldiers. They looked so subdued. We were all between twelve and twenty years of age. We arrived at a little forest, where there was a camp controlled by the French. It was in the Zone Turquoise, in Gikongoro.

For about three months, this FAR soldier came anytime he wanted and raped me. He would take me from one of the tents in the camp to a nearby forest, outside the camp, where no one could see us. When the young Hutu man raped me for the first time in that house, I screamed and shouted, but when I was raped in the forest, I did not say a word. I had accepted what was happening to me and realized that I didn't have a chance to escape.

About three hundred women and girls were at the camp. The soldiers just picked whomever among us they wanted to rape. The French knew what was happening and did nothing to prevent it. The rapes sometimes took place right in front of their eyes. Rather than protecting Tutsi, the French were helping the Hutu, and towards the end of the genocide, the Zone Turquoise was used by many Hutu as an escape route from Rwanda to the DRC.

Emmanuel was not the only soldier who raped me. Another soldier raped me multiple times in his house outside the camp. He was nicknamed Rukokoma. When the FAR soldiers learned that the RPF were approaching, they moved the camp to another area within the Zone Turquoise. That is when Rukokoma found me. For the four days we stayed at this second location, Rukokoma forced me to be his "wife."

As the Inkotanyi were approaching, the FAR soldiers burned their uniforms and started wearing normal clothes so they would look like civilians. One day I was able to go to a nearby Red Cross post, where they provided me with some biscuits, food, blankets, oil for cooking and medicines. I told the doctor what was really happening in the little forest. That same night, the Inkotanyi attacked the place and took all the FAR soldiers away with them. Some of the FAR soldiers were re-educated and later joined the RPF. The girls and women were taken to a secure place.

For me, the genocide did not end after the Inkotanyi rescued us from the camp. For about two years, Rukokoma, who pretended to be a civilian not involved in the genocide, forced me to stay in the "marriage." We remained in Gikongoro until I was six months pregnant with his child. At this point, he fled to the DRC, since he had become more and more afraid I would tell the RPF about his true identity. I don't know where he is now. In January 1997, I gave birth to a girl, but I hated her, because she was a constant reminder of what had happened to me. I didn't breastfeed her because of that, though the doctors pressured me to forget about the past and to feed her.

In 2003, I found out who killed my father. The man's name is Hussen. Before appearing in *gacaca* court, he wrote a letter from prison confessing to the murder and to other crimes. He asked for forgiveness only to avoid a longer sentence in *gacaca*. Our government had installed a policy that encouraged *génocidaires* to confess to the crimes they committed, in order to achieve justice and reconciliation among Rwandans. This would help genocide survivors learn what had happened to their loved ones and where their bodies lay, so that they could receive a proper reburial. It would also ease the enormous caseload for the courts, which needed to process the cases of around 800,000 *génocidaires*. A confessing *génocidaire* would, in return, receive a reduced sentence. However, Hussen managed to flee when he was temporarily released before appearing in *gacaca*, and I don't know where he is today.

Because I wasn't able to go to school, I am now forced to cultivate the land, even though I am weak because of my HIV status. I eat some of the food that I grow myself and sell the rest at a nearby market. Even though I am frail, I have to farm in order to survive and to take care of my daughter and my sick mother, who live with me. It is my biggest wish that someone can help me farm the fields, so that I can have a better life.

A few years ago, I was desperate and lonely, but after meeting with other survivors, I felt comforted and helped. An organization provided me with food and antiretroviral treatments. I received counselling and was able to consult a doctor. When I first found out that I was HIV positive, in 2000, I refused to take the antiretroviral treatment, because I wanted to die. I am happy now that I have taken the treatment, since it is better for my health. Other rape survivors who were on antiretroviral treatment comforted me and inspired me to take the medicine. If it weren't for the treatment, I would probably not have been able to cultivate the land any longer.

I have not forgiven those who killed my family, those who raped me or even those who took our possessions. I go to the *gacaca* courts, but I am more and more frightened to give my testimony when I see what happens to other survivors when they do so. They are intimidated or, even worse, killed. I wonder why I should give my testimony, because the Interahamwe are being released. It seems that our testimonies in *gacaca* courts are more formalities than truly helpful.

The international community abandoned us in 1994. If the international community is still denying the realities and atrocities of the genocide, then they are still killing us. Maybe our testimonies will help them open their eyes. Maybe. We are still hurting, and we wish someone would notice.

BÉATRICE MUKANDAHUNGA

BORN: May 12, 1973
BIRTHPLACE: Mata, Gikongoro

IT IS HARD for me to accept the fact that I am HIV positive. I live in awful conditions. I owned a bakery after the genocide, but in 2007 I was robbed and I could not continue my business. I lost one sister and one brother during the 1994 genocide. As the oldest of my surviving family, I have to take care of my three sisters and my cousin and pay for all their things, including their school supplies and clothes.

Before the genocide in 1994, I had only completed primary school. My father worked at a tea manufacturing plantation, and my mother was a farmer. In 1959, years before I was born, discrimination against Tutsi began, and my father and his sister left the country to go to Burundi. In Rwanda, houses that belonged to Tutsi were burned, and Tutsi were killed. My father returned in 1970, because he wanted to start his own life in Rwanda and no longer wanted to live with his sister, who had gotten married. Although there was still discrimination against Tutsi, he made a vow to himself never to flee Rwanda again, even if Hutu tried to kill him.

My parents married in 1971 and started a large family. I had, in all, eight brothers and sisters. When I was born, my father called me Mukandahunga, which means "the daughter of the one who fled the country." He called one of my sisters Nshutininka, which means "a friend is a cow," because every time Hutu were jealous of my father's land or his cows, he would give a cow to those who had the power to protect him. Cows are a sign of deep friendship in our culture.

There were many Hutu in our community, which was called Mata. In April 1994, when I was still living with my parents, Hutu started burning Tutsi houses. In my community, the rampaging started on April 8, at my uncle's house. Because my uncle had nine strong sons, the one Interahamwe militiaman who went there could not overpower them with his machete. That man left to round up some friends, and my uncle's family took the opportunity to flee to the Catholic church of Kibeho, which was about two hours away from my uncle's house in Gikongoro.

On April 10, a Hutu named Innocent came to our house and warned us not to seek refuge at the church in Kibeho or at schools in our area, because we would be killed if we did so. This was not the first time a Hutu had helped us. In 1992 and 1993, another Hutu man warned us that the killing of Tutsi was about to begin. He helped us because my family had given him some cows. So on April 10 my entire family except for one sister, who decided to stay at Kibeho thinking it would be safer, spent the night in a sorghum field. Early the next morning, we walked to Butare. The genocide had not yet started there. Although we considered walking to Burundi, we decided to stay in Butare, since it seemed safe. We tried our luck with a rich Tutsi man who lived in Butare. He welcomed us into his house, and we believed that his wealth would spare him and us. But two days later, the Interahamwe militia came and killed the rich Tutsi man and his son.

There were many Tutsi at the rich man's house, and when the Interahamwe attacked, we all ran away in separate directions. Except for two of my brothers, my family spent the night at the home of my aunt, who was also Tutsi and who lived in Butare. Although the genocide had still not really started yet in Butare, Interahamwe militia from Gikongoro had been sent to begin the killings, and we left my aunt's house the next day, since we thought we would not be safe there. My father and uncle stayed on, believing they could fight the Interahamwe. I never saw them again, and I do not know how or where they were killed.

We fled to a nearby church in Karama. Only a few minutes after we got there, a bus full of FAR soldiers and Interahamwe arrived. The rest of us wanted to flee, but my mother refused, believing we would not be killed. When the shooting started, we insisted that we should leave. My mother said she wanted to stay, as she would die anyway, but when we told her we would stay too and die with her, she agreed to leave with us.

As we fled, we got separated from each other because of the shooting. Still, I was not far behind my mother and my younger sister. Together with many other Tutsi, we ran through a small alley. My mother was one of the first to arrive at a roadblock set up by Interahamwe, and she was hacked to death. Since she was wearing nice clothes, they stole those from her body. My sister, also in the front line of the fleeing Tutsi, was wounded by machetes at this roadblock, too. I was able to escape the horrors at that roadblock because of the chaos. I ran towards the centre of Butare town, because I had heard it was safe there. Others fled in the direction of Burundi.

I arrived at the Anglican church of Butare, where many Tutsi from Gikongoro were hiding. There I was approached by some FAR soldiers from ESO, a training centre for FAR soldiers in Butare, who were hand-picking young girls to abuse. The soldiers were looking for girls who already had breasts, since they considered them old enough to rape. Girls in the church were cutting off their hair so that the soldiers would not think they were old enough. The FAR soldiers took some other girls and me to their small houses in the ESO compound near the church. We were mostly teenagers.

I was raped all night long. The soldier who first raped me told me to cooperate; he said otherwise it would be much worse, as he would use more force against me. He told me it was the end of all Tutsi, but if I cooperated, he might help me survive. He raped me three times that night. Over the following days, I did not care what those soldiers were doing to me, because I wished to die. Six of us girls were raped by those soldiers day and night. There were many different men who raped me on different days. After the rapes, some girls were sent back to the church. Others were swapped between soldiers to be raped further, and some were even killed. Although I was in so much pain when I was first raped, I didn't feel anything afterward. It didn't matter any longer, since I felt I was going to die anyway.

Minister Pauline Nyiramasuhuko, who was the minister of Family and Women's Affairs in Rwanda and lived near the church in Butare, oversaw the "work" of the genocide at the church some of the time. She said she did not want to see "dirt" in the fields. We overheard one soldier reporting this to another soldier on his walkie-talkie. On the order of the minister, buses arrived to take us to Nyaruhengeri, just outside Butare, to be killed there. The girls on the first two buses did not survive the ride. I was on the third bus. When we arrived in Nyaruhengeri, the Interahamwe militia said they were exhausted from killing. They told Minister Nyiramasuhuko that there were too many dead bodies already, and that the smell of the corpses was so disgusting that she would have to send people to take the corpses back to Butare before they would agree to continue their "work." The minister said she could not promise them that, so we were taken back to Butare in order to be killed there.

The bus then took us to Rango forest, near Butare. There we were "welcomed" by a group of Interahamwe militia who raped us again and again for one week. There was a big ditch where they planned to throw us after they were done with us, and where many dead bodies from previous killings already lay. I was raped three times, by different men. Two girls, named Kantarama and Francine, died after enduring more sexual and other abuse than they could handle. We were raped, day after day, until the day the Inkotanyi arrived in Butare. A white priest had informed the RPF of our location. As soon as the Interahamwe heard that the RPF were on their way to the forest, they fled.

The RPF took us from the forest to a refugee camp in Butare. I stayed there for one week, until the conflict was over, and then for another week in a school called Groupe Scolaire Officiel de Butare. Some time later, I met my younger sister and a cousin who had survived the genocide, and we chose to live together. We lived in Butare for one year and after that we moved to Kigali.

After the genocide, I hated all Hutu, hated churches and hated praying. I wanted to hurt the Hutu, but I could not, because they were much stronger than I was. I learned that I was HIV positive in 2005, when I was about to get married. When I found out, I lost all hope, and none of the spiritual healing I had experienced since 1994 helped. The man I was about to marry did not want to marry me when he found out about my HIV status. I have now decided that I will marry only if the man is also HIV positive. I have no children, but I do not want to die before I have them. Even with my health status, I could have a baby without infecting the baby with HIV.

My sisters don't know that I am sick. They are very traumatized themselves, and I don't want to shock them. I have never asked them whether they were also raped during the genocide, but they are married and not sick like me. I don't want any pity or gossip. If people find out I am HIV positive, they might change their manner towards me. They might not greet me any more or might reject me completely.

I decided to share my testimony so that every country in the world knows genocide took place in Rwanda. I hope that everyone who hears my story helps us to find treatment for our sicknesses. I have forgiven those who hurt me. I do not remember them, and I would not recognize even one of them if I met him on the street. I don't go to the *gacaca* courts, because there is no justice in *gacaca* courts. The thought of those courts disturbs me. The courts are far away from where I live, and I have no money for bus tickets to go there. I also do not feel safe there. When I started praying and started to forgive the rapists, I felt no need to go to *gacaca* courts any longer. I actually don't really have a choice: it is hard to hate someone you don't even know. I just wish to have a normal life.

FRANÇOISE KAYITESI

BORN: 1962 (date and month unknown)
BIRTHPLACE: Bicumbi, near Kigali

M Y MOTHER AND father left Rwanda when I was just two years old. My father was a secretary in the royal court and therefore an important personality. When the discrimination against Tutsi began, he was in great danger, because Hutu believed he held the secrets of the court. The year my parents fled Rwanda, Tutsi were being burned alive in their houses. My parents had not planned to leave, but some kind Hutu warned them about the dangers of staying. My father fled to Uganda, and my mother, who was also Tutsi, to Burundi. My mother, my uncle and I began the journey to Burundi together, but my mother grew too tired to take me along. My uncle decided to stay with me in Rwanda, because he was not really wanted by the killers. My parents planned to return for me at some later stage, but I never saw my father again.

When I was a bit older, I moved from my uncle's house in Bicumbi, just outside Kigali, to Gatsata quarter in Kigali. I lived in a community where Tutsi were a minority, but this situation didn't seem to influence our relationships. We had friends among Hutu as well as Tutsi, though the discrimination was more visible in our schools. Tutsi students did not have the right to perform better than Hutu students did. For example, our teachers would switch the names of Tutsi who had received better marks with the names of Hutu who had not performed as well. I was a good student but did not continue my studies as I had hoped, because my place in secondary school had already been taken by a Hutu. Instead, I learned how to sew, cook and take care of children. I also studied auto mechanics and learned French by taking a language course. After I finished this training, I studied management, which included courses on how to use a typewriter.

I went to work in a garage in Gatsata called Amesorwa, owned by a Hutu from Gisenyi, where I did the typing and sold car parts. My husband and I met on the streets in Kigali, where he traded clothes for a living. We realized later that our parents had once been neighbours, though we didn't recognize each other at first. We got married in 1980.

I managed to see my mother twice while she was in exile in Burundi. In 1989, right after I had returned from a visit to see her, people came to my home to interrogate me about whether I had cooperated with the *inyenzi*. I had already burned my *laisser passer* card, which stated my ethnicity, so that they could not accuse me of being an RPF spy. The owner of the garage where I worked occasionally chauffeured Interahamwe to their meetings. But when the militia came to humiliate the Tutsi who worked in his garage, the owner was always by our side. He did not protect us out of compassion, but because he could not afford to lose hard-working people.

The owner of the apartment we rented in Kigali used to persecute us as well. My husband and I did not have a key to the front gate, whereas other renters did. The apartment owner used to tell my younger brother, who lived with us, that he would cut off his long nose, which was considered a typical Tutsi feature. We always had to return home earlier than others so that we could enter the apartment before the owner locked the front gate.

In 1991, Tutsi could not walk the streets, because there was a lot of hostility towards us. There were Congolese soldiers who had supposedly come to help the FAR soldiers protect Rwandans from an RPF invasion, but all they did was enter houses to rape Tutsi women. During that period, there were many barricades on the streets, and identity cards were checked for ethnicity. While my husband and I contemplated going to Burundi, we did not have the money to leave.

When I learned about the death of Habyarimana on the radio, I thought it would be our time for peace and justice, because Habyarimana was a dictator. But I realized I was wrong when I heard people screaming and shouting in the streets early in the morning. After several hours, a group of Interahamwe militia came to our home with guns, machetes, swords and other weapons. They beat my housemaid, who was Tutsi, after she showed them her identity card. I gave them money and begged them to let us live. They accepted and left. Because we knew they would return, my three sons and I ran from our home as soon as the militia were out of view and went to the home of our neighbours. My husband ran to hide in the bushes, because our neighbours did not want to hide him. It was much more dangerous to help a Tutsi man than a Tutsi woman.

After three days, my neighbours heard that the RPF were getting closer, and they ordered us to leave their house. I decided to walk with my sons to Gitarama. We travelled with another neighbour, a beautiful twenty-three-year-old girl. On our way to Gitarama, we were stopped by Interahamwe and FAR soldiers positioned at a roadblock before the bridge crossing the Nyabarongo River. They were asking people for their identity cards and killing the Tutsi. In the large crowd of people at the roadblock, I saw my husband. I believe the Interahamwe threw him into the river moments after, though I am not sure. Some people managed to escape when the Interahamwe and FAR soldiers were arguing with each other and not paying attention. I escaped with my children, who were small enough to pass through the legs of the militia and the soldiers.

My sons, our neighbour and I continued on our way, cutting through small forests until we finally arrived in Nyanza, my husband's birthplace. There, we hid on a cassava plantation until three Interahamwe found us. As soon as I saw them I completely lost my mind and could no longer think. They said that they wanted to kill us but first they wanted to "taste" a Tutsi woman. They raped me one after the other, in front of my children. They also raped my neighbour. While they were raping us, the Interahamwe kept saying that we Tutsi should have stayed in Ethiopia. After they were finished, they tied me to a tree, beat my children, calling them the sons of cockroaches, and abandoned us. The next morning I felt very ill, and my belly hurt. I drifted constantly in and out of consciousness. I was tied to the tree for three days before my neighbour had the strength to untie me.

As we continued our journey, hiding along the way, my three-year-old son became ill and eventually fell into unconsciousness. An old lady I didn't know gave us some milk. When I fed that to him, he started breathing normally again. But with the aid of their dogs, the Interahamwe who had raped us found us hiding in the forest. Two of them took me to a muddy area in a clearing and shouted at me to lie down. Many militiamen raped me, while holding their weapons beside them, yelling that my friends the Tutsi and the Inkotanyi should come and save me if they wanted to. My neighbour was also raped many times. Fortunately, my children were far away from the clearing and could not hear or see what was happening.

After the Interahamwe finished raping me, they left me, and I reunited with my children in the forest. A girl passed by and offered to help by taking my two older children to a nuns' orphanage. The girl gave my sons some girls' clothing to wear, so that they would have a better chance of survival. My youngest son stayed with me, because I could still pretend he was a girl.

In May, my youngest son and I arrived in Gikongoro. For several weeks, we hid in bushes and empty houses, never for longer than two days at a time. We would flee whenever we heard footsteps, and we managed to conceal ourselves before the Interahamwe noticed us. Weeks later, the RPF reached that area and helped us to return home to Kigali. When they first arrived, I was afraid of them, because I was not sure whether they were RPF or government soldiers. After a few days, as I saw them distributing clothes and food and speaking to other Tutsi in a nice way, I realized that they were really there to help us.

Back in Kigali, I learned that my brother had not survived. He had been killed on the first day he returned to our apartment. The Interahamwe, who included one of our former neighbours, had stabbed my brother with a sword. His blood was splashed all over the walls of our apartment. He had been able to run as far as the main road before they caught him and buried him alive.

Shortly after the genocide ended, I realized that I was pregnant. Everyone told me to abort the pregnancy, because I didn't know if the father was my husband or one of the men who had raped me. But I couldn't bring myself to do it. Something stopped me. I prayed that the baby belonged to my husband and not an Interahamwe. When my son was born, in January 1995, I counted back the days and realized that he was conceived during the time I was still with my husband. A few months after my son's birth, I saw that he looked like my husband, too.

In 2003, I found out that I was HIV positive. I was always ill and I experienced severe pains in my private parts. Because I tested HIV positive, my doctor advised me to bring my four children in to be tested, too. My youngest son tested HIV positive. When I first found out that I had HIV, I completely lost hope. I thought it would be my last few days on Earth. I prayed a lot. No one knew but my sons, who survived the genocide with me. I have no one else. My husband, his family and most of my own family were killed during the genocide.

After the genocide, I could not return to the garage to work, because my boss had fled the country. I started typing letters for people on a rented typewriter. That provided me with some income to care for nine children, including five orphans I had adopted—my four nephews and one niece, as well as my mother, who had returned to Rwanda in the fall of 1994.

Since the genocide, I have headaches and feel permanently ill. I am constantly afraid. I hallucinate and see knives in front of my eyes all the time. When I go to buy meat, I sometimes imagine that the butcher is going to kill me with his knives. Every time I try to fall asleep, I see the men who raped me, telling me to take off my clothes. I feel like I can never experience joy, and I do not wish to speak about what I experienced. I can't even write down what happened to me. When I try, I stop after one page and burn the writing. Worst of all, I have been rejected by my community because my neighbours know that I am HIV positive. They always insult me about my HIV status. Maybe they would stop rejecting me if they knew I was infected from the rapes I endured during the genocide. I keep on praying, because prayers have helped make my life worth living. I also discovered from other survivors that if I take antiretroviral treatment, together with enough food, I will be able live longer.

I don't feel that I forgive the Interahamwe, not yet. No one has asked for my forgiveness, and no one wants to talk about it. I still live among them, and the very best I can do is ignore them. I wouldn't have the courage to accuse those who raped me in the *gacaca* courts, but I know that even if I did, they would not receive the punishment they deserve. I couldn't accuse the ones who raped me even if I wanted to, since those rapes happened far from Kigali, and I don't know who those men are. When killers confess to their crimes, they are quickly released. I would rather see them in prison for the rest of their lives. Although I have attended *gacaca* three times, each time I go I become very traumatized, seeing myself being raped in the forest again. I think that the people who are now released from prison should help the survivors of the genocide by building them houses and digging their fields. If I was a judge, I would sentence them to carry out general works to help the community.

Today, I wish to find a job so that I will have a regular income and can live in better conditions. My eldest son still remembers what happened during the genocide, though he hardly talks about it and he never speaks about the rapes he saw perpetrated against his mother. I do not wish for my face to be recognizable for the portrait in this book—not to protect myself, but for my children, because I do not want to create more wounds in their hearts. I decided to share my testimony so that the world may know what happened to us in 1994. We must never let this happen again and must build a better world for our children.

ERNESTINE NYIRANGENDAHAYO

BORN: 1981 (day and month unknown)
BIRTHPLACE: Muyira sector, Butare

M Y FATHER WAS a Tutsi my mother was seeing while she was still married to a Hutu man. Because I was illegitimate, my Tutsi mother sent me to live with my grandparents in Muyira sector, near Butare, as soon as I was born. The rest of my family also lived there. I had two half brothers who were Hutu, but I didn't get along with them, because I was Tutsi and grew up in a Tutsi family. After my mother divorced her husband, she came to live with my grandparents and me, but she never ended up marrying my father.

I spent my childhood helping to shepherd my grandparents' cattle. The Tutsi were in the minority in our area. The Hutu could do anything they wanted, like "asking" Tutsi for cattle to slaughter. If a Tutsi refused, the Hutu would take the cattle anyway and never be held accountable for it. I remember an incident in 1993 when a Tutsi man refused to give one of his cows to a Hutu. Later that evening, the Hutu went to the man's house with a machete and killed the man and his entire family. That was before the genocide.

When the genocide began in our neighbourhood, I was in the pasture taking care of my cows. After I witnessed Interahamwe burning Tutsi alive in their houses, I left the cows in the pasture and ran to Nyamure mountain, only a few minutes from where I was. Many Tutsi families had gathered at Nyamure mountain, and the Interahamwe approached with machetes and guns. They shot so many people that I was covered in blood and the Intera-hamwe thought I was also dead. I fell unconscious. When I woke up, there were dead bodies all over the mountain, but the Interahamwe were no longer there. I was covered with the blood of my aunt, uncle and grandmother, but I was not wounded myself. Everywhere I looked I saw dead bodies, thousands of bodies. I felt nothing and thought that I would die anyway.

I couldn't stay there because of those bodies. Late in the night, I left Nyamure mountain and hid in a nearby cornfield. The next morning, an old Hutu man—I think he owned the field—found me hiding and took me with him. He told me that he would not hurt me but would hide me. I trusted him and followed him to his house.

The old man had two sons, who were about twenty-three and twenty-six years old and were both Interahamwe. When the sons saw me coming, they exchanged a look, but at the time it did not occur to me that the look was not normal. I took a shower and went to bed immediately. Two days later, when I woke up, the old man was already out, occupied with stealing Tutsi property. His sons, who were still at home, asked me if I was a boy or a girl. I knew that boys were killed immediately, so I didn't object when they asked me to take off my clothes to see if I was lying about being a girl. One of them then said that I was too young to be raped—I was only thirteen years old at the time—but the other one said that even if I was too young, my vagina would not be. They told me that they would kill me after raping me. I saw that they had knives, so I begged them to stab me to death immediately. I wanted to die, but they said they would kill me only after they were finished with me.

One of the men pushed me onto the bed and told me that my shouting wouldn't save me. I screamed very hard, because I was in so much pain, but when he finished, his brother came on me and raped me, too. Fortunately, when their mother, a Tutsi, came home, they left me in the room. She did not reprimand her own sons, because she was afraid they would kill her too. When she saw me bleeding, she took me to some sort of cave just outside the house, where the family stored their bananas. My vagina smelled very bad, and she washed me with warm water and gave me some food. She said that this was every Tutsi's destiny and that she was afraid for her own life, too. She told me not to go back to the house, because her sons would kill me. I spent four days in that cave and decided to leave only when I heard

Ernestine in front of her house with her mother and her two children

that the Inkotanyi were approaching. I feared the fighting that would probably ensue. I waited for the Hutu family to leave the house, and then I left the cave.

While I was fleeing, I met one of my aunts, who was with her three-year-old son. We continued on together. There were also many Interahamwe fleeing. There was panic everywhere, but we finally reached the Nyanza football stadium. We crossed paths with a group of Interahamwe in the stadium, and one of them told my aunt to dig three holes, which would be our graves. She started digging, and after she finished, the Interahamwe beheaded my cousin with a machete. They ordered my aunt to sit in the hole and they beat her with nailed clubs before one of them chopped her head off, too. While they were beating her, an old Hutu lady I didn't know pushed me into a nearby tent, where the Interahamwe did not find me.

The old lady said that she was going to help me escape and that I might be the only Tutsi survivor. It was no longer safe to stay at the stadium, because many Tutsi were being killed. I went with the old lady. She told me that I was too young to die, and she felt compassion for me. She herself was married to a Tutsi man. She hoped that someone would do for her own relatives what she was doing for me. We didn't know where we were going, but when we finally arrived in Gikongoro, we spent two weeks there. We were living in horrible conditions. We slept outside, we had nothing to eat, and we were always begging for food.

After the RPF liberated the country, I tried to reach my home. I travelled with the old lady, who happened to live near the mountain where my family members had been killed. I found out that my mother was still alive. The rest of my family had died.

After the genocide, I lived in terrible conditions and experienced many ailments in addition to the trauma. In 2002, I married a man named Emmanuel. He was a friend of a relative of mine, and he first came to my house in 2001. He liked me and came more often. He knew what had happened to me during the genocide, but he comforted me and decided to marry me anyway. He was also a Tutsi who had experienced the genocide, and that is why he understood what had happened to me.

I gave birth to our first child, a boy, in 2003. I continued feeling ill after that, and I went for an HIV test, which came back positive. I was tested for HIV many times and in many different places, because I wanted to verify whether I was truly HIV positive, especially since I was pregnant at the time. I believe I was infected with HIV when I was raped during the genocide. When my husband found out I was HIV positive, he did not leave me, which is a miracle. I have several tumours on the outside of my private parts, and I don't know what to do. Because of the antiretroviral treatments I'm taking, I feel slightly better. I gave birth to a second child, a daughter, in 2005. Luckily, neither of my children is HIV positive.

The men who raped me are all dead. They were killed by the Inkotanyi. I don't know if I would have forgiven them if they were still alive, but I don't think so. The fact that the Interahamwe are being released makes me feel bad, but we don't have any choice but to accept it. I would have preferred to know that they were still in prison or even dead. I hope that my testimony will open some human hearts and make people feel there is something they can do. Even if they don't have material things to offer, their presence or their thoughts would be a nice thing. It helps us to know that people are thinking of us.

3

LIFE AFTER "DEATH"

THE DEVASTATING CONSEQUENCES of conflict continue long after hostilities have ended. In the case of Rwanda, the after-effects of the sexual violence inflicted on women and girls during the genocide have been particularly severe. With so many of their loved ones dead, many of these women and girls have had to forge a solitary path. Their own communities, and often the remaining members of their families, have shunned them because of the stigma associated with rape and HIV. Kept on the outskirts of society and living among former *génocidaires*, survivors are easy prey for retaliation by perpetrators hoping to silence truth and prevent their victims from implicating them for their past horrific deeds. Survivors face not only social isolation but appalling poverty, as well as continuing physical and psychological trauma from the indescribable brutality they suffered and witnessed.

In many cases, the grief and trauma afflicting these embattled women are further compounded by the burden of caring for the injured and the orphaned. And even before the memory of genocide had begun to fade, many women bore children conceived as a result of rape. Although some women resorted to self-induced abortions, an estimated two thousand to fifteen thousand "children of hate," or *enfants mauvais souvenir* ("children of bad memories"), were born after the genocide.[1]

Rape and other acts of violence carried out in the scope of war also considerably increase women's vulnerability to sexually transmitted diseases.

HIV and other sexually transmitted infections have been described as "the legacy left to women raped during the genocide."[2] Women and girls are especially vulnerable to HIV infection during periods of conflict, since families and communities are broken up and displaced. The injuries that often result from rape, such as tearing and abrasions, further increase victims' risk of infection.[3] In Rwanda, the HIV prevalence rate in rural areas increased dramatically, from 1 per cent before the onset of the genocide to 11 per cent in 1997.[4]

Even in the absence of sexual violence, vulnerability to HIV infection can increase significantly during conflict. Damage to a country's health infrastructure can result in the inability to adequately sterilize equipment, and it limits access to testing facilities and resources such as post-exposure preventive treatment and social services. Health care providers may be unable to care for survivors, to mitigate the damage done or to reduce the likelihood of infection from future sexual encounters. For those who are HIV positive, conflict may also disrupt access to HIV treatment, care and support. Most of the survivors interviewed for this book did not receive medical treatment after rape, and one survey revealed that only 6 per cent of respondents who were raped during the genocide had ever sought medical treatment.[5] Reasons for this may range from the unavailability or inaccessibility of health facilities and the barrier the stigma of rape presents, to the reality that treatment was not likely a priority with so many other challenges confronting rape survivors. When treatment for Rwandan rape survivors has been provided, it has been characterized as "too little, too late."[6]

Today, survivors continue to experience significant gaps in access to health care. Only an estimated 28 per cent of Rwandan households affected by HIV/AIDS are able to afford basic health care, and many decide to forego it altogether.[7] A 2008 UN report revealed that only 53 per cent of adults in need of antiretroviral treatment are receiving it.[8] Even where treatment and support are available, the stigma attached to an HIV-positive status has impeded many Rwandans from using those services.

Ironically, while many survivors living with HIV lack access to medical treatment and a basic standard of well-being, those accused of high-level participation in the genocide awaiting or undergoing trial at the International Criminal Tribunal for Rwanda receive antiretroviral treatment

Pascasie *(centre)* with other survivors during a gathering at Solace Ministries in Kigali

and health care in prison.[9] Though a policy was implemented in 2004 to provide antiretroviral treatment for witnesses and potential witnesses, treatment is available only to the few who testify. With access to anti-retroviral treatment and health care already a problem, women and girls also bear the largest burden of care for family members. This is particularly true in post-genocide Rwanda, where the majority of survivors are women. Girls, for their part, are more likely to be taken out of school to tend to sick relatives than are boys. Thus, not only are women uniquely at risk of HIV infection during and after conflicts, they are very often responsible for caring for family members with HIV/AIDS.

Poverty, as mentioned, is an additional constraint on women's ability to reclaim their lives after rape.[10] Of Rwandan families living in poverty, 60 per cent are headed by women. Overall, 34 per cent of women lead households in Rwanda, of which widows constitute 21 per cent.[11] Women's experiences of poverty may be more acute than those of men because of a number of gender-based forms of exclusion. For instance, although women in Rwanda play a greater role in agriculture (93 per cent of farmers are women), women continue to experience difficulty owning land and other farming assets, regardless of legal changes that technically permit women's ownership.[12] Not surprisingly, sexual violence endured during the genocide is linked to the feminization of poverty. For many women, the physical and psychological trauma they experienced during the genocide means they are no longer able to work. Survivors who have been widowed are often left without family income. The additional responsibility created by other family members who are unable to work plunges those households into extreme poverty.[13] Even when survivors are capable of working, their HIV status can lead to stigma and discrimination, loss of employment, difficulty in asserting property rights and other human rights violations.[14]

The scarcity of basic needs and the lack of economic opportunities for women render women and girls more likely to engage in sex in exchange for food, shelter or services. Insecure living circumstances, including unprotected housing, further expose women to unwanted sexual advances from neighbours and passersby. Both sets of circumstances pose additional risks of HIV infection. Though women in Rwanda are among the most highly educated in the region,[15] feminized poverty remains a great challenge.

Despite the calls to "never again" permit the horrors of the Rwandan genocide to occur, an alarming number of women and girls continue to endure sexual violence in the genocide's aftermath. Among Rwandan women, 31 per cent have experienced physical violence, most often from a husband or partner, and 13 per cent have experienced sexual violence.[16] Domestic violence, or the threat of it, has been linked to HIV infection, in part due to women's inability to refuse sex, to negotiate safer sex or to leave violent relationships. In the first three months of 2007, rape was the most widely reported crime in Rwanda, even though rape is consistently underreported.[17] These figures unveil the reality that sexual violence remains a fact of life for women across Rwanda.

SURVIVORS IN RWANDA want accountability. They wish to see the perpetrators of the genocide brought to justice. Survivors also need treatment for
the many health problems still ailing them; stable housing; employment;
a secure future for their children, free from the lingering threat of genocide; and a sense of belonging and community. The Rwandan government,
local and international organizations, and local and international courts
all have a role to play in healing the wounds survivors bear. Though the
world community has been slow to take action, sexual violence is increasingly being recognized as an issue that requires a long-term, multifaceted
response. Years after the genocide, have survivors' needs been addressed?
What can we learn from Rwanda?

THE RWANDAN GOVERNMENT'S RESPONSE

Since the genocide, there have been a number of positive legislative
changes in Rwanda, including laws that guarantee women and girls the
same rights as men and boys to inherit property. The 2003 Rwandan
Constitution provides equal protection under the law for all, as well as
protection against discrimination, including discrimination on the basis
of sex or HIV status.[18] In August 2006, the Rwandan Parliament considered legislation to punish gender-based violence.[19] During debate on the
bill, parliamentarians recognized the urgent need to address the high incidence of gender-based violence in Rwanda and its strong relationship with
poverty. They also acknowledged that violence against women obstructs
efforts to attain gender equality and noted that Rwandan society had come
to tolerate, even accept with impunity, acts of violence against women.[20]

Although Rwanda's existing penal code prohibits and punishes rape,[21]
prosecutions are rarely pursued. Inadequate police training in the effective
investigation of sexual assault and the absence of a standard protocol for
conducting such inquiries have reportedly led to inconsistent court ver-
dicts, confusion among law enforcement and government officials, and
inattention to sexual violence against women.[22] In May 2005, a "Gender
Desk" was created within the Rwandan National Police to deal with some
of these problems. Police have been trained to address sexual and gender-
based violence, and the Gender Desk offers a nationwide toll-free telephone
service for reporting these crimes. According to the United Nations Development Fund for Women (UNIFEM), in 2006 the Gender Desk enabled the

Marie Jeanne *(far left)* and Marie Claire *(left)* with other survivors in Kigali

Rwandan Police to refer 1,777 rape cases for prosecution, resulting in 803 convictions.[23] Nevertheless, national legislation that clearly identifies and provides redress for violence against women has not been implemented. At the time of writing, the bill on gender-based violence had yet to become final law.[24]

Rwanda's genocide law recognizes rape and sexual torture as acts of genocide and as crimes against humanity, punishable by a maximum term of life imprisonment.[25] Along with crimes committed by the planners and supervisors of the genocide, rape and sexual torture are recognized as category one crimes, or crimes deemed to be the most severe and the highest priority for prosecution.[26] Under an amended genocide law of 2008, the semi-traditional *gacaca* courts, presided over by individuals with "high integrity" elected from the community, began to try the alleged perpetrators of rapes committed during the 1994 genocide.[27] Prior to this amendment, *gacaca* courts had jurisdiction to deal with all crimes related to the genocide except category one crimes, which were slated for prosecution before national courts. In light of the enormous number of individuals accused of category one crimes, however, and the amount of time required to process these cases before national courts, cases of sexual violence not yet prosecuted, involving some 6,808 persons, were redirected to *gacaca* courts. One notable feature of the *gacaca* is the training provided to *gacaca* judges on how to interact with survivors of sexual violence in court. Trials involving sexual violence are also required to proceed in closed session to protect survivors from stigmatization and intimidation by community members supporting the accused.[28] In addition, the genocide law of 2008 stipulates that trauma counselors must be available for survivors of sexual violence, to help them cope with their past experiences and the trial process itself.

However, when survivors find the courage to come forward, the justice system too often fails to guarantee their physical security. Between 1995 and mid-May 2008, about 167 genocide survivors were murdered.[29] Witnesses, judges and members of the *gacaca* courts have also been targeted. Accordingly, many survivors express fear of attending *gacaca* because of the threats of intimidation and/or death at the hands of those related to the accused *génocidaires*. Many also point out that the *gacaca* does not provide them with a sense of justice; many rapists receive short sentences and are already being released into the community in exchange for their confessions.

While compensation might further help to address survivors' needs, it is virtually impossible to obtain this remedy in Rwanda. National courts have awarded monetary claims to victims, but since offenders did not have the financial means to pay the victims, they have simply avoided payment.[30] The Fund for Assistance for Genocide Survivors (FARG), funded by the Rwandan government, has also been largely inadequate in meeting the needs of survivors. The fund's main contributions have been in the areas of education, health and housing; assistance to women and girls who survived sexual violence during the genocide is not a high priority.[31] Moreover, community service, a form of redress requiring *génocidaires* to work on community reconstruction projects, is applicable only to category two offenders.[32] Consequently, many women and girls have lost all hope of reparation or assistance, either from convicted offenders or from the government.[33]

THE RESPONSE BY NON-GOVERNMENTAL ORGANIZATIONS

In Rwanda, survivor-led and survivor-run organizations abound, in large part due to the absence of government and other services, but also because survivors understand the unique needs of their peers with regard to care, treatment and support.[34] Solace Ministries grasped early on the complex dimensions of the struggles facing women, realizing that successful management of HIV infection would require more than medication. HIV-positive survivors of sexual violence require counselling and therapy for post-traumatic stress, nutritious food to maintain their health, stable housing, education about their illness, effective treatment, income-generating training, and resources such as school fees and materials to support the children and orphans they care for.

Human rights and development organizations do not always view attention to the emotional and spiritual health of survivors as crucial. In a post-conflict environment where psychiatric treatment is not easily available, Solace Ministries offers individual and peer counselling, support groups and home-based care. Material support is provided in the form of sustainable, income-generating activities and, for those affected by HIV, antiretroviral treatment. Women derive a sense of security from being among other survivors, as well as a reprieve from the stigmatization many experience in their communities. At Solace, survivors obtain their medication and receive counselling in a space where they feel at ease. An unexpected result of individual and group counselling has been the formation of close-knit support networks among survivors, as survivors who have learned ways to deal with their trauma counsel those who are still struggling. The experience of Solace Ministries demonstrates that providing effective HIV care, treatment and support to survivors of genocidal rape requires integrating medical care with psychosocial, material and other support while addressing barriers such as poverty and stigmatization. This grassroots empowerment model may serve women and children experiencing ongoing mass rape and sexual violence in other conflicts as well.

Beneficiaries of Solace Ministries during a meeting in Kigali

The international community has responded to the needs of survivors of the Rwandan genocide in diverse ways, with varying success. Foreign governments and international organizations have contributed to the reconstruction of the country in spite of, or perhaps due to, their inaction in 1994.[35] One of the first legal responses was the establishment of the International Criminal Tribunal for Rwanda (ICTR) in 1994. More recently, the UN General Assembly adopted a resolution in 2008 calling for an end to sexual violence globally. International initiatives to promote reparation for survivors of sexual violence post conflict have also been mobilized.[36]

THE INTERNATIONAL CRIMINAL TRIBUNAL FOR RWANDA

This is not rape out of control. It is rape under control. It is also rape unto death, rape as massacre, rape to kill and to make the victims wish they were dead. It is rape as an instrument of forced exile, rape to make you leave your home and never want to go back. It is rape to be seen and heard and watched and told to others; rape as spectacle. It is rape to drive a wedge through a community, to shatter a society, to destroy a people. It is rape as genocide.[37]

CATHARINE A. MACKINNON, "Rape, Genocide and Women's Human Rights"

The ICTR was established in Arusha, Tanzania, in late 1994 to prosecute the masterminds of the Rwandan genocide: government officials, military leaders, the clergy and media heads. The tribunal, which has jurisdiction over crimes committed in 1994, defines rape as a crime against humanity and as a war crime. This marked one of the earliest instances in international criminal law in which rape was recognized as a stand-alone crime rather than a private consequence of conflict with no real need for punishment.[38] Since the tribunal's establishment, it has rendered thirty-seven judgements.[39] Only eight cases have involved the successful prosecution of sexual violence.[40] Nevertheless, the tribunal was responsible for a remarkable breakthrough in its recognition of rape and sexual violence as acts of genocide, a precedent that acknowledged these crimes could rise to the threshold of "destroying a group," namely the Tutsi, by, for example, "causing serious bodily or mental harm."[41]

The tribunal has also received its fair share of criticism. Several women who testified there felt revictimized, in large part because of the disclosure of some details of their identity by defence counsel.[42] In a number of cases, family, friends and neighbours in Rwanda who were unaware of a witness's past rejected and isolated her upon her return to the community. Outlandish and sexist questioning by defence counsel in court also led to the retraumatization of some survivors.[43] Survivors of sexual violence are prevented from expressing their views and concerns during proceedings and are only permitted to appear as witnesses to corroborate the prosecutor's case.

Another major concern expressed by women who testified before the tribunal, especially those infected with HIV, has been their lack of access to medical treatment, while perpetrators are provided with antiretroviral treatment and nutritious food to help them cope with the disease in prison.[44] Despite several efforts by the ICTR prosecutor to include individual compensation for victims in the tribunal's mandate, ICTR judges remained unconvinced.[45] Finally, the fact that the tribunal is geographically far removed from the Rwandan population and has no effective outreach program has prevented its staff from explaining the tribunal's mandate or purpose to survivors of the genocide. Though the tribunal may have made considerable strides in the field of sexual violence in international criminal law, it remains debatable whether it has, in the eyes of survivors, achieved justice or reconciliation.[46]

THE UN SECURITY COUNCIL RESOLUTION TO END SEXUAL VIOLENCE IN CONFLICT

On June 19, 2008, the UN Security Council adopted Resolution 1820 to end sexual violence in conflict. The resolution demands, among other things, that parties involved in armed conflict cease committing acts of sexual violence against civilians and take appropriate measures to protect civilian women and girls from all forms of sexual violence. The resolution also acknowledges that, despite repeated condemnation, violence and sexual abuse of women and children trapped in war zones are not only ongoing but, in some cases, so widespread and systematic as to "reach appalling levels of brutality." The resolution notes that women and girls are particularly targeted by sexual violence, which is used in some cases as "a tactic of war to humiliate, dominate, instil fear in, disperse and/or forcibly relocate civilian members of a community or ethnic group." Resolution 1820 underscores the vital importance of women's participation in preventing

conflict, maintaining peace and security, and building peace post conflict. Significantly, the resolution excludes crimes of sexual violence from
amnesty accords as part of peace negotiations and underlines the importance of ending impunity for such crimes.

Nevertheless, it is not the dearth of international instruments or other
guidelines that has undermined the rights of girls and women in situations
of conflict. It is clear that international criminal law already recognizes
rape in its various forms as a crime. Rather, the failure thus far of national
governments and the international community to address sexual violence
is reflective of their general reluctance to treat sexual violence with the seri-
ousness it deserves. Still, Resolution 1820 lays to rest debate about whether
or not the Security Council should address sexual violence in conflict
situations. The institution possesses significant moral authority, and its
pronouncements do carry weight, even though their implementation has
often been a challenge.[47]

ONLY RECENTLY HAS the world recognized sexual violence as a devastating form of harm and one that its perpetrators must account for. This
recognition has been achieved largely through women speaking out about
their experiences of rape. Although many survivors have understandably
kept silent about the horrors they have endured, others have bravely made
themselves heard, calling for sexual violence to be criminalized and for the
crime to be viewed in the broader context of women's empowerment.

Sexual violence does not occur in a vacuum. In both wartime and peace
time, it is linked to gender inequality and rooted in a pervasive culture of
discrimination. The experience of Rwanda has taught us that sexual violence not only has grave physical, psychological and health consequences
for its victims, but also perpetuates a tolerance of abuse against all women
and girls. An unresolved climate of impunity threatens women's security
by subjecting those who are already struggling to survive to a generalized
environment of fear. A climate of impunity also distresses survivors, who
feel a sense of injustice because their perpetrators have never been held
fully accountable. To address sexual violence in a systemic way, we must
re-evaluate cultural practices and judicial systems to ensure that they are
inclusive and protect women against all forms of abuse. Laws must be
developed that deal both with violence and with issues that affect women's

An elderly *gacaca* judge resting after rejecting the appeal of a *génocidaire* rights in all spheres, such as property, inheritance, marriage and divorce. Creating a world free from sexual violence requires creating conditions where justice can flourish and strong laws can be enforced through a strong judicial system. Tackling the issue requires the combined efforts of national and international governments, judiciaries, media, and civil society and non-governmental organizations.

Rwanda's population was 70 per cent female immediately following the genocide. Given this demographic imbalance, women have assumed previously inconceivable roles as heads of households, community leaders and financial providers.[48] Women occupy 56 per cent of the seats in Rwanda's parliament—the highest proportion in the world—and they are well represented at various levels of government.[49] Women also account for 55 per cent of the workforce[50] and own 41 per cent of Rwandan businesses.[51] Empowering women can rejuvenate post-conflict economies and serve to fight poverty.[52] Women, far more than men, invest profit in the family, renovate homes, improve nutrition, increase savings and spend on children's education.[53] Because they have not been implicated in the genocide to the same extent as men, women in Rwanda have also been entrusted with the tasks of reconciliation and reconstruction, and they are recognized as agents of change, with meaningful roles to play in the recovery and reintegration of their families and communities.[54]

Women are building the future of Rwanda, but sexual violence is an issue that still urgently requires attention. Enabling survivors to speak without fear or shame about their experiences is imperative. Survivors' stories also remind us to remain vigilant against the sexual violence that threatens women both in and outside of conflict situations. Many survivors, however, must have their basic needs met before they can begin the process of healing and speaking out. The international community can contribute by raising awareness of sexual violence, mobilizing national governments into action and contributing to reparation initiatives and justice projects. Survivors of sexual violence are a living testament to our collective abandonment of them, but they also represent the promise of transformative change. We cannot afford to turn our backs on them again.

NOTES

1. The lower figure is based on an estimate by the UN. See UN Commission on Human Rights, *Report on the Situation of Human Rights in Rwanda* (see part 1, note 3), and UN Population Division, *Abortion Policies: A Global Review* (New York, June 2002). Save the Children, an international children's rights organization, however, estimates the number of women impregnated as a result of rape during the genocide to be much higher: 15,000. See Andrew Lawday, *HIV and Conflict: A Double Emergency* (London: Save the Children, 2002), p. 5, citing Esther Mujawayo and Mary Kayitesi Blewitt, "Sexual violence against women: Experiences from AVEGA's work in Kigali" (paper presented at the Silent Emergency Seminar, London, June 1999).

2. See African Rights, *Rwanda, Death, Despair and Defiance* (London: African Rights, 1994), p. 448.

3. Women are more susceptible than men to infection from HIV in any given heterosexual encounter because of the greater area of mucous membrane exposed during sex in women, the greater quantity of fluids transferred from men to women, the higher viral content in male sexual fluids and the microtears that can occur in vaginal or rectal tissue from sexual penetration. See World Health Organization (WHO), "Gender Inequalities and HIV," www.who.int/gender/hiv_aids/en (last accessed August 31, 2008).

4. See *Sexual violence in conflict settings and the risk of HIV*, Violence against Women and HIV/AIDS: Critical Intersections no. 2 (Geneva: UNAIDS and WHO, 2004). This figure has declined again to 3 per cent in 2005. See Republic of Rwanda, UNGASS *Country Progress Report*, p. 14 (see part 1, note 27).

5. See Jeanne Ward, *If Not Now, When?: Addressing Gender-Based Violence in Refugee, Internally Displaced, and Post-Conflict Settings: A Global Overview* (New York: Reproductive Health for Refugees Consortium, 2002).

6. See African Rights, *Rwanda: Broken Bodies, Torn Spirits: Living with Genocide, HIV/AIDS and Rape* (Kigali, 2004).

7. See Pia Schneider and others, *Paying for HIV/AIDS Services: Lessons from National Health Accounts and Community-Based Health Insurance in Rwanda, 1988–1999* (Geneva: UNAIDS, 2001), p. 7.

8. See Republic of Rwanda, UNGASS *Country Progress Report*, p. 30.

9. See Anne-christine d'Adesky, "Rape OutRAGE: Why is an army of rapists getting HIV meds, while its victims are left to die?" *POZ Magazine* 94 (2003), www.poz.com/articles/169_656.shtml (last accessed January 29, 2009); and Amnesty International, Rwanda: "Marked for Death," p. 20 (see part 1, note 7). See also the discussion of the International Criminal Tribunal for Rwanda below, notes 44 and 45.

10. After the genocide, for example, inheritance laws barred surviving women and girls from accessing the property of their dead male relatives unless they had been explicitly named as beneficiaries. As a result, thousands of women were left with no legal claim to their homes and their land. Although a new law has enhanced women's rights to inheritance and land ownership, most women are still discriminated against in this respect and continue to live in extreme poverty. See Amnesty International, Rwanda: "Marked for Death," pp. 4–5, 9.

11. See Faith Malka and Serge Musana, "Rwanda: Eradicating Poverty—Develop a Woman, Develop a Nation," *The New Times*, July 16, 2008, http://allafrica.com/stories/200807170032.html (last accessed January 29, 2009). According to Malka and Musana, the African average for woman-led households is 20 per cent.

12. Chiseche Mibenge, "Gender and ethnicity in Rwanda: On legal remedies for victims of wartime sexual violence," in *Gender, Violent Conflict and Development*, ed. Dubravka Zarkov (New Delhi: Zubaan Books, 2008), p. 158.

13. See African Rights, *Rwanda: Broken Bodies, Torn Spirits*.

14. See Amnesty International, *Rwanda: "Marked for Death,"* p. 2.

15. See Republic of Rwanda, UNGASS *Country Progress Report*, p. 15.

16. With 12 per cent of Rwandan women reporting experiencing emotional violence, altogether more than one-third of Rwandan women have experienced physical, sexual and/or emotional violence. See National Institute of Statistics of Rwanda, *Rwanda Demographic and Health Survey 2005* (Kigali, 2006), p. 177.

17. See Republic of Rwanda, UNGASS *Country Progress Report*, p. 15.

18. See Claire Devlin and Robert Elgie, "The Effect of Increased Women's Representation in Parliament: The Case of Rwanda," *Parliamentary Affairs* 61 (2008): 237–54; and WE-ACTX, *Know Your Rights!: A Community Handbook on Health-Care Rights and Other Laws* (Kigali: WE-ACTX for Hope, 2007), downloadable from www.we-actx.org/community-legal/ (last accessed January 29, 2009).

19. The title of the bill is the "Draft Law on the Prevention, Protection and Punishment of Any Gender Based Violence."

20. See Irene Zirimwabagabo, "Gender-Based Violence Bill Passes in Rwandan Parliament," UNIFEM *News*, August 7, 2006, www.unifem.org/news_events/story_detail.php?StoryID=502 (last accessed August 31, 2008).

21. In Rwanda, rape is primarily seen as a crime committed by a man against a woman, that is, the forced penetration of the sexual organs, anus or mouth by a male sexual organ or other object. The crime is punishable by a sentence of five to ten years, or ten to twenty years for rape committed against a minor under the age of sixteen. The sentence may be doubled for certain prescribed aggravating circumstances, such as the accused holding a position of authority, multiple perpetrators or serious physical harm. These aggravating circumstances are likely to be present in times of war. See Articles 358–62 of Rwanda's penal code.

22. According to Human Rights Watch, the denial of "adequate procedural protections, including confidentiality and access to female police officers and judicial officials trained in dealing with cases of sexual violence" puts survivors of rape at further risk of stigmatization and retraumatization. See Human Rights Watch, "Rwanda: Rape Survivors Find No Justice," *Human Rights News*, September 30, 2004, www.hrw.org/english/docs/2004/09/30/rwanda9391.htm (last accessed August 31, 2008); and Jennie Burnet, "Rwanda," *Countries at the Crossroads 2007*, p. 10, www.freedomhouse.org/uploads/ccr/country-7259-8.pdf (last accessed August 31, 2008).

23. See Letitia Anderson, "GBV Offices—A Sign of Progress in UNIFEM Partnership with Rwandan Police," UNIFEM *Gender Issues*, April 18, 2007, www.unifem.org/gender_issues/voices_from_the_field/story.php?StoryID=588 (last accessed November 30, 2008); and Rwanda National Police, "Police Gender Desk," www.police.gov.rw/news.php?id_article=32 (last accessed November 30, 2008). In August 2008, a Gender Desk was also launched within the Rwandan Ministry of Defence to deal with sexual and gender-based violence in Rwanda and within the Ministry's peacekeeping missions. Since its

inception, the Gender Desk has conducted training on women's human rights and gender-based violence for military personnel, civilians and people trained as "gender focal points" at the district level. While the Gender Desk seems to be a positive step to combat violence, its impact has yet to be measured. See "Rwanda Defence Force Officially Launches Gender Desk," UNIFEM News, August 13, 2008, www.unifem.org/news_events/story_detail.php?StoryID=712 (last accessed November 30, 2008).

24. The bill had passed both houses of Parliament, but still awaited the president's signature. At the time of writing, the Rwandan government had only committed to elaborating a national policy on gender-based violence and violence against women. See H.E. Prof. Joseph Nsengimana, Permanent Representative of Rwanda to the United Nations, statement at the Security Council Open Debate on Women and Peace and Security: Sexual Violence in Situations of Armed Conflict, New York, June 19, 2008, www.peace-women.org/un/sc/Open_Debates/Sexual_Violence08/Rwanda.pdf (last accessed August 31, 2008).

25. The first genocide law for Rwanda was implemented in 1996 and amended in 2000 and 2001. It was replaced by the genocide law of 2004, which was amended on several issues in 2006, 2007 and 2008. Although the current genocide law does not provide a definition of "genocide" or "crime against humanity," the definitions in the Statute of the International Criminal Tribunal for Rwanda (described below) can provide guidance. In short, genocide entails the commission of acts such as killing or causing serious bodily or mental harm, with intent to destroy, in whole or in part, a national, ethnic, racial or religious group. Crimes against humanity include crimes such as torture, rape and enslavement when these are committed as part of a widespread or systematic attack against any civilian population on national, political, ethnic, racial or religious grounds. The general difference between genocide and crimes against humanity is that, where crimes against humanity are concerned, the specific intent to destroy a group of people is absent. For the genocide law of 2004, see Republic of Rwanda, *Organic Law No. 16/2004 of 19/6/2004 establishing the organisation, competence and functioning of Gacaca Courts charged with prosecuting and trying the perpetrators of the crime of genocide and other crimes against humanity, committed between October 1, 1990 and December 31, 1994.*

26. To complement the genocide law's recognition that rape is primarily committed against women, the term "sexual torture" comprises the mutilation of men's sexual organs. See Chiseche Mibenge, "Gender and ethnicity in Rwanda," pp. 162–63. The genocide law also encompasses category two crimes (e.g., murder and torture not carried out by the planners and supervisors of the genocide) and category three crimes (property offences).

27. See "1994 Genocide: Gacaca Courts Will Start Trying Rape Cases Next Month," *Hirondelle News Agency,* June 25, 2008, www.hirondellenews.com/content/view/2170/26/ (last accessed January 29, 2009). After the genocide, the Rwandan government adapted the traditional *gacaca* courts (which had previously dealt primarily with family disputes) to preside over crimes related to the genocide in order to expedite the trials of some 800,000 currently identified alleged *génocidaires*. Prosecution of this number of people before national courts would have taken an estimated 100 years. See the National Service of Gacaca Jurisdictions summary of persons prosecuted for genocide on the *Inkiko-Gacaca* Web site at www.inkiko-gacaca.gov.rw (last accessed August 30, 2008). Approximately 12,000 *gacaca* courts are operating throughout the country. Although the courts have been heavily criticized in the West because of an alleged lack of respect for the rights of the accused, no better alternatives have been

proposed. With the speed at which the *gacaca* courts are currently proceeding, Rwandan authorities hope to have most of their cases completed by 2009. For a discussion of the Western criticism of the courts, see Human Rights Watch, *Law and Reality: Progress in Judicial Reform in Rwanda* (New York, 2008) and Amnesty International, *Rwanda: Gacaca: A Question of Justice* (London, 2002).

28. The obligation for survivors of sexual violence to testify in closed session was first introduced in the genocide law of 2004. The 2008 genocide law, which amended the 2004 genocide law, sanctions members of the *gacaca* court for revealing details of closed sessions. Sanctions range from one to three years in prison. This measure is intended to discourage individuals involved in a trial from discussing the case outside the courtroom and to encourage more survivors of sexual violence to participate. See Republic of Rwanda, *Organic Law No. 13/2008 of 19/05/2007, Organic Law modifying and complementing Organic Law No. 16/2004 of 19/6/2004 establishing the organisation, competence and functioning of Gacaca Courts charged with prosecuting and trying the perpetrators of the crime of genocide and other crimes against humanity, committed between October 1, 1990 and December 31, 1994 as modified and complemented to date.*

29. See "Rwanda Ibuka Report—167 Genocide Survivors Murdered Since 1995," *Hirondelle News Agency*, July, 15 2008. The study revealed that some 64 of the 167 recorded victims were reportedly poisoned, and 103 others were killed by firearms, traditional weapons, strangulation or burning.

30. Although Articles 27–32 of the 1996 genocide law, *Organic Law on the organisation of prosecutions for offences constituting the crime of genocide or crimes against humanity committed since 1 October 1990*, recognized a victim's right to compensation, that law is no longer in force. The current genocide law does not include provisions for victims' compensation because those who were convicted pursuant to the 1996 genocide law were too poor to pay damages to victims; decisions were rendered that could not be executed. According to a report by the International Crisis Group, close to US$100 million had been awarded after only 4,000 people had been tried, but not a single cent has been paid out, because the defendants are all indigent. See International Crisis Group, *International Criminal Tribunal for Rwanda: Justice Delayed*, Africa Report No. 30 (Nairobi/Arusha/Brussels, 2001), p. 33.

31. The law establishing FARG does not analyze the violations women faced, and there is consequently no attention paid to the needs of survivors. See Coalition for Women's Human Rights in Conflict Situations, "Women's Right to Reparation" (background paper, Nairobi Meeting, March 19–21, 1997), p. 61.

32. See Republic of Rwanda, *Organic Law No. 10/2007 of 01/03/2007, Organic Law modifying and complementing Organic Law No. 16/2004 of 19/6/2004 establishing the organisation, competence and functioning of Gacaca Courts charged with prosecuting and trying the perpetrators of the crime of genocide and other crimes against humanity, committed between October 1, 1990 and December 31, 1994 as modified and complemented to date, article 14.*

33. See Penal Reform International, *From Camp to Hill, the Reintegration of Released Prisoners*, Research Report on the Gacaca No. 6 (London, 2004), p. 55. See also "The Limitations of Justice Without Compensation," *Hirondelle News Agency*, April 18, 2005. There have also been reports that funding for the FARG has been misused. See James Munyaneza, "Ministers discuss FARG, order audit," *The New Times*, June 19, 2006, www.rwandagateway.org/article.php3?id_article=2010 (last accessed January 29, 2009). Although in 2006 the Minister of Justice proposed a new fund to replace the FARG, this suggestion has not yet been implemented. See Felly Kimenyi, "Govt to replace FARG," *The New Times*, September 29, 2006, www.rwandagateway.org/article.php3?id_article=3098 (last accessed January 29, 2009). In the same year, the president of Ibuka, the umbrella organization of all genocide survivors'

organizations in Rwanda, requested that the government's budgetary allocation to the FARG be raised to 12 per cent from 5 per cent, an amount that would enable survivors of the genocide to live in humane conditions. See James Munyaneza, "IBUKA writes to Speaker over FARG," *The New Times*, June 14, 2006, www.rwandagateway.org/article.php3?id_article=1969 (last accessed January 29, 2009).

34. The appendix to this book lists a number of national and international organizations working with survivors of sexual violence.

35. See the budget summary on Rwanda on the USAID Web site, www.usaid.gov/policy/budget/cbj2006/afr/rw.html (last accessed August 31, 2008), for an overview of the many international donors still operating in Rwanda.

36. The *Nairobi Declaration on Women's and Girls' Rights to a Remedy and Reparation* was adopted on March 21, 2007. The declaration is based on the conviction that women and girls who survive sexual violence will never obtain justice if the programs for reparation supposedly serving them are not designed and directed by those principally concerned. The declaration aims to bring solutions to the systematic failings inherent in national initiatives for truth and reconciliation, as well as to improve the mechanisms for reparation being developed by the International Criminal Court.

37. See Catharine A. MacKinnon, "Rape, Genocide and Women's Human Rights," *Harvard Women's Law Journal* 17 (1994): 5–16.

38. The International Criminal Tribunal for the former Yugoslavia, which has jurisdiction over genocide, crimes against humanity and war crimes committed in countries that were part of the former Yugoslavia as of 1991, was established in 1993. It also defines rape as a crime against humanity.

39. This is the status as of October 29, 2008. The tribunal in Rwanda is expected to close its doors at the end of 2009, by which time it will have prosecuted about 89 persons. Some of the current and outstanding indictees will have their cases transferred to a national jurisdiction, such as Rwanda, willing to proceed with the case. About half of the cases involve charges of sexual violence.

40. This is the status as of October 29, 2008. In a number of cases, charges of sexual violence were dropped or the accused was acquitted. See also Anne-Marie de Brouwer, *Supranational Criminal Prosecution of Sexual Violence: The ICC and the Practice of the ICTY and the ICTR* (Antwerp and Oxford: Intersentia, 2005).

41. The tribunal held that the rapes committed during the genocide "resulted in physical and psychological destruction of Tutsi women, their families and their communities" and that "sexual violence was a step in the process of destruction of the Tutsi group—destruction of the spirit, the will to live and of life itself." Even though neither rape nor sexual violence was explicitly recognized in the definition of genocide, the *Akayesu* case clarified once and for all that the commonly understood interpretation of genocide as exterminating a group was not the only way to commit a genocide. See *The Prosecutor v. Jean-Paul Akayesu* (see part I, note 23).

42. For a more complete account of the achievements and shortcomings of the Rwanda tribunal, see Binaifer Nowrojee, "Your Justice Is Too Slow": Will the ICTR Fail Rwanda's Rape Victims? UNRISD Occasional Paper Series No. 10 (Geneva: UNRISD, 2005); and Anne-Marie de Brouwer, *Supranational Criminal Prosecution of Sexual Violence*.

43. Questions such as "Did you touch his penis?" or insinuations that a survivor could not have been raped because she hadn't bathed for a long time were posed by defence counsel solely to revictimize and attack the dignity of the woman being questioned.

44. It should be noted that since 2004 the tribunal has provided not only general medical services to witnesses testifying at the tribunal (including potential witnesses) but also antiretroviral treatment for those in need.

45. In the view of the ICTR judges, the tribunal was established primarily to prosecute persons responsible for serious violations of international humanitarian law. The additional task of dealing with compensation claims, they held, would take too much time and effort and further delay trial proceedings. See Anne-Marie de Brouwer, *Supranational Criminal Prosecution of Sexual Violence.*

46. The International Criminal Court (ICC), which was established in 1998 and has been operative since 2002, also deals with the main perpetrators responsible for crimes committed in conflict situations and is permanent in nature. Notable differences between the ICC and the ICTR are the greater number of crimes of sexual violence recognized by the ICC and ICC provisions that allow victims to participate in the proceedings and request reparation. These positive changes in international criminal law were partly inspired by the shortcomings of the ICTR. At the time of writing, the ICC was investigating and prosecuting crimes committed in northern Uganda, Darfur, the DRC and the Central African Republic. Charges of sexual violence have been made against a number of suspects and those accused.

47. The Security Council is also the body of the United Nations charged with responsibility for maintaining international peace and security. It is therefore within its purview to act against states waging unlawful wars and to outline the roles of UN peacekeeping forces.

48. See Elizabeth Powley, "Strengthening Governance: The Role of Women in Rwanda's Transition—A Summary" (presented at the UN Office of the Special Adviser on Gender Issues and Advancement of Women, Expert Group meeting on enhancing women's participation in electoral processes in post-conflict countries, January 19–22, 2004, Glen Cove, NY), www.un.org/womenwatch/osagi/meetings/2004/EGMelectoral/EP5-Powley.PDF (last accessed August 31, 2008).

49. See, for example, "Female-majority parliament hopes to lead Rwanda forward," *Rwanda Development Gateway*, October 7, 2008, www.rwandagateway.org/article.php3?id_article=10024 (last accessed October 25, 2008); and Felly Kimenyi, "Rwanda: Parliament Gets Female Speaker," *The New Times*, October 7, 2008, http://allafrica.com/stories/200810070732.html (last accessed January 29, 2009). Rose Mukantabana made history as the first woman in the African Great Lakes region to become Parliamentary Speaker, the sixth in Africa and thirty-first in the whole world, according to the Inter-Parliamentary Union.

50. See Anthony Faiola, "Women take charge in Rwanda," *The Guardian Weekly*, June 13, 2008.

51. See World Bank, "Doing Business 2008," press release, September 26, 2007, http://go.worldbank.org/X38QR84WN0 (last accessed August 30, 2008).

52. See Anthony Faiola, "Women take charge in Rwanda."

53. See Anthony Faiola, "Women take charge in Rwanda."

54. See Elizabeth Powley, "Strengthening Governance." According to Powley, women represent only 2.3 per cent of genocide suspects in Rwanda.

AFTERWORD

He poured milk on me to see if a Tutsi really was a cat.

They put a nailed club in my vagina . . . Whenever they saw a dog, the police forced me to call it by my father's name.

The French were helping the Hutus rape us . . . Sperm in my nose . . .

Told us we looked like snakes, like cockroaches . . . He left me in my ragged underwear.

I discovered I was HIV positive.

These men tried to cut my vagina into two parts with a sword in order to share me . . . I buried myself in the bloody corpses . . . None of those who harmed me have ever faced real justice.

I have not received any kind of compensation since the genocide . . . The soldiers killed what I would have become.

RAGMENTS, RAPE SHRAPNEL, images, sensations that lodge forever in the body, in the soul.

These testimonies are unbearable. The acts of hatred and violence unimaginable. The resiliency and kindness of the survivors beyond grace.

I do not feel forgiving. I feel angry. I feel insane with outrage. Almost fifteen years have passed since the genocide in Rwanda, and I have just returned from the Democratic Republic of Congo, where I spent weeks interviewing women who have survived these same sexual atrocities of war. Many were attacked by the same bands of militia documented in this book. Call it a mad grab for natural resources, call it tribal warfare, call it the outcome of a history of colonialism, racism and manufactured ethnic divisions, but right now the war is being fought on the bodies of women. Rape, torture, humiliation, HIV, vaginal destruction. Cheaper than AK-47s or grenades or scud missiles, rape is biological warfare. It not only wounds women in the moment it occurs, but it lodges forever in consciousness, in body, in communities, in families. From my first trip to Bosnia during the war of the 1990s, in which twenty to fifty thousand women were raped, through the recent horrors in Zimbabwe, I have witnessed the impact of femicide all over the planet. And I have witnessed the bizarre, inexplicable indifference of the international community, of governments, of the United Nations to truly respond to this crisis.

Women are the primary resource of our planet. If they are destroyed, with them so is our future. If they are violated and desecrated anywhere on this earth, we are all violated and desecrated.

The brave survivors in this book have come forward with dignity and strength to reveal their faces and their scars. They are asking for justice. They are hoping that their testimonies will have an impact and make change. I urge you to be disturbed by what you have read, really disturbed. And then I urge you get angry, get bold, become determined to do everything in your power to end this heinous violence everywhere in the world. End this violence that sustains gender inequality, that keeps the world deeply and perilously imbalanced, forever at war. End this violence that gives global licence to the destruction of women, that is the end of life itself.

EVE ENSLER
December 11, 2008

WHAT YOU CAN DO

MANY SURVIVORS OF the genocide in Rwanda are still struggling to make ends meet. Here is a list of organizations in and outside of the country that make a difference in the lives of those who survived sexual violence. All of these organizations welcome donations, and some have sponsorship programs that allow donors to support individual survivors.

SOLACE MINISTRIES is an ecumenical, survivor-run organization that supports widows, orphans and survivors of sexual violence. The survivors featured in this book are all beneficiaries of Solace Ministries.
Solace Ministries
P.O. Box 6090, Kigali, Rwanda
tel +250-08-305094 (Jean Gakwandi, Director)
mucyo@rwanda1.com
www.solacem.org

IBUKA ("REMEMBER") is the umbrella organization for Rwandan organizations supporting survivors of the genocide. As such, it can also provide information about organizations that specifically support survivors of sexual violence.
Ibuka
P.O. Box 625, Kigali, Rwanda
info@ibuka.org
www.ibuka.net

MUKOMEZE ("EMPOWER HER") offers a sponsorship program specifically for women and girls who survived rape and other forms of sexual violence during the genocide. Mukomeze partners with Solace Ministries in Rwanda.
Mukomeze
Cimburgalaan 72, 4819 BD Breda, The Netherlands
tel +31-(0)6-14282748
info@mukomeze.nl
www.mukomeze.nl

SURVIVORS FUND helps survivors of the Rwandan genocide deal with and recover from the tragedies of 1994, supporting a wide range of services for victims in Rwanda and assisting survivors in the U.K.
Survivors Fund (SURF)
10 Rickett Street, West Brompton, London UK SW6 1RU
tel +44-(0)20-7610-2589
info@survivors-fund.org.uk
www.survivors-fund.org.uk

WOMEN FOR WOMEN INTERNATIONAL provides women survivors of war, civil strife and other conflicts with tools and resources to move from crisis and poverty to stability and self-sufficiency.
Women for Women International
4455 Connecticut Ave NW, Suite 200, Washington, DC USA 20008
tel +1-202-737-7705 · fax +1-202-737-7709
general@womenforwomen.org
www.womenforwomen.org

WOMEN'S INITIATIVES FOR GENDER JUSTICE advocates for accountability before the International Criminal Court for gender-based crimes and crimes of sexual violence.
Women's Initiatives for Gender Justice
Anna Paulownastraat 103, 2518 BC The Hague, The Netherlands
tel +31-(0)70-302-9911 · fax +31-(0)70-392-5270
info@iccwomen.org
www.iccwomen.org

THE CANADIAN HIV/AIDS LEGAL NETWORK promotes the human rights of people living with and vulnerable to HIV/AIDS in Canada and internationally, through research, legal and policy analysis, education, advocacy and community mobilization.
Canadian HIV/AIDS Legal Network
1240 Bay Street, Suite 600, Toronto, ON Canada   M5R 2A7
tel +1-416-595-1666 · fax +1-416-595-0094
info@aidslaw.ca
www.aidslaw.ca

THE STEPHEN LEWIS FOUNDATION funds community-based initiatives in Africa focussing on women, orphans, grandmothers and people living with HIV/AIDS.
Stephen Lewis Foundation
260 Spadina Avenue, Suite 501, Toronto, ON Canada   M5T 2E4
tel +1-416-533-9292 · fax +1-416-850-4910
info@stephenlewisfoundation.org
www.stephenlewisfoundation.org

V-DAY is a global movement dedicated to ending violence against women and girls.
V-Day
303 Park Avenue South, Suite 1184, New York, NY USA   10010-3657
www.vday.org

DIGNITAS INTERNATIONAL increases access to effective HIV/AIDS prevention, treatment, care and support in resource-limited settings through community-based solutions.
Dignitas International
2 Adelaide Street West, Suite 200, Toronto, ON Canada   M5H 1L6
tel +1-416-260-3100 · fax +1-416-260-3170
info@dignitasinternational.org
www.dignitasinternational.org

GLOSSARY

AIDS: Acquired Immune Deficiency Syndrome. AIDS is a syndrome result-ing from the damage to the human immune system caused by the Human Immunodeficiency Virus (HIV). When HIV infection becomes advanced, it is often referred to as AIDS.

antiretroviral treatment: Also called ARV treatment. Treatment for people living with HIV that works by inhibiting the ability of HIV to reproduce in the body.

bazungu: Kinyarwanda for "white people."

bourgmestre: Term used in 1994 for the mayor of a commune. The *bourgmestre* was the most powerful figure in the commune, subject to the authority of the prefect.

cockroach: Term used by Hutu to insult Tutsi.

commune: In 1994, Rwanda was divided into twelve regional prefectures that were further subdivided into communes.

conseiller: Term used in 1994 for the head of a sector.

DRC: The Democratic Republic of Congo, also commonly referred to as the Congo, formerly known as Zaire.

FAR: Forces Armées Rwandaises, or Rwandan Armed Forces, the national army of Rwanda until July 1994.

FARG: Fonds d'Assistance aux Rescapés du Génocide, or Fund for Assis-tance for Genocide Survivors, established by the Rwandan government to assist survivors of the genocide in obtaining housing, education and health care.

gacaca: Kinyarwanda for "on the grass," referring to the traditional courts of Rwanda. Their mandate evolved after 1994 to adjudicate crimes committed during the genocide.

gender-based violence: Violence that specifically targets women or disproportionately affects women. Includes but is not limited to sexual violence.

genocide: The deliberate and systematic destruction, in whole or in part, of an ethnic, racial, religious or national group. The term was first used at the 1948 UN Convention on the Prevention and Punishment of the Crime of Genocide.

génocidaire: A person who commits or has committed the crime of genocide.

HIV: Human Immunodeficiency Virus. HIV is a virus that attacks the body's immune system and can lead to AIDS. Someone who is diagnosed as being infected with HIV is said to be HIV positive.

ICTR: The International Criminal Tribunal for Rwanda based in Arusha, Tanzania. Established in 1995 by a UN Security Council resolution to prosecute the main perpetrators of the Rwandan genocide.

Inkotanyi: Kinyarwandan term used to refer to the Rwandan Patriotic Front, or RPF. Hutu extremists often used this term to refer to alleged Tutsi spies.

Interahamwe: Kinyarwanda for "those who attack together." Refers to a Hutu militia group, composed mainly of Hutu youth, that was active during the genocide.

inyenzi: Kinyarwanda for "cockroach." A term used by Hutu to insult Tutsi.

kangura: Kinyarwanda for "wake others up," and the title of a magazine, established in 1990 and published in Kinyarwanda and French, that stoked ethnic hatred in the run-up to the genocide.

Kinyarwanda: The national language of Rwanda, spoken by Hutu, Tutsi and Twa.

laisser passer card: Travel document used in Rwanda in lieu of a passport.

Opération/Zone Turquoise: Opération Turquoise was a military operation in Rwanda under the mandate of the United Nations. During the genocide, Zone Turquoise was the French-controlled "safe zone" in the southwest of Rwanda. The French have been accused of assisting Hutu *génocidaires* during the genocide.

prefect: Term used in 1994 for the head of a prefecture.

prefecture: In 1994, Rwanda was divided into twelve regional prefectures, each governed by a prefect. On January 1, 2006, the twelve prefectures of Rwanda were abolished and replaced with five provinces.

Presidential Guards: Elite force under the command of the Rwandan president.

Radio Muhabura: A pro-Tutsi RPF radio station, created in 1991, that broadcast from RPF-occupied territory, including Uganda.

RPF: Rwandan Patriotic Front, a political and military movement formed in 1987 by the Tutsi refugee diaspora in Uganda. Beginning in 1959, Tutsi refugees fled to Uganda to escape ethnic purges. In 1994, the RPF invaded Rwanda and halted the genocide. The RPF, led by President Paul Kagame, is the current ruling political party of Rwanda.

RTLM: Radio Télévision Libre des Mille Collines. A Hutu-controlled radio station famous for broadcasting propaganda against the Tutsi.

Rwandan franc: Currency used in Rwanda. At the time of writing, one U.S. dollar was equivalent to approximately 550 Rwandan francs.

sector: A subdivision of a commune.

sexual violence: Violence encompassing various forms of sexual abuse, such as rape, gang rape, sexual mutilation and sexual slavery. Sexual violence is a form of gender-based violence.

snake: Term used by Hutu to insult Tutsi.

UNAMIR: United Nations Assistance Mission for Rwanda, established in October 1993 to help implement the peace agreement between the Rwandan government and the RPF. UNAMIR's mandate and strength were adjusted several times during the genocide. Its mandate ended in March 1996.

ACKNOWLEDGEMENTS

TO THE SEVENTEEN survivors featured in this book, and to the countless others who have shared their stories with us in Rwanda, there are no words to express our appreciation for your courage and our admiration for your perseverance and dignity. You are our partners in this book and our teachers and friends in life.

This book would also not have been possible without the many wonderful people and organizations who have assisted us along the way. These include the staff at Solace Ministries, who welcomed us with open arms. Despite their many commitments in providing assistance to survivors of the genocide, each staff member made time for us. In particular, director Jean Gakwandi believed in this project from the beginning and did everything in his power to guarantee its success. Denise Uwimana was instrumental in having the survivors recount their stories. Mama Lambert, who became our mentor and our inspiration, empowered the survivors to share their experiences and performed a miracle or two to rectify derailed plans. Our translators, Jessie Gakwandi and Doris Uwicyeza, displayed sensitivity, professionalism and endless patience and endurance, and for this we thank them.

Cordaid provided us with the resources to forge ahead on schedule, and we thank Sanne Bijlsma for making this possible.

Thanks to our publishing team at D&M Publishers Inc. for their professionalism; to Scott McIntyre, who believed in this project and shared our vision; and to Barbara Pulling for her expertise and wisdom in helping to mould our final product. Thanks also to Stephen Lewis, Eve Ensler, Purva Panday and Christina Magill for agreeing to support this project so whole-heartedly in spite of their harried schedules.

A special thanks to Freek Dekkers for his unwavering support, to Kim Seidl for her photography mentorship, to Jen Sookfong Lee for her insight and encouragement, and to Bernice and Christian Paul for their passionate, enthusiastic promotion of the book and its accompanying Web site.

Finally, we thank our families—Jef, Leonie, Vanessa, Nick, Ria, Hans, Oi, Ho-Ming, So-Ching, Hui-Tong, Vincent, Angie, Karen, Siham, Zaki, Sina, Najat, Jawad, Najat and Abdul-Hussein—for their generosity, uncon-ditional love and support.

ANNE-MARIE DE BROUWER is an associate professor of international criminal law at Tilburg University, The Netherlands, whose work in Rwanda has focussed on women's rights. She is the founder of Mukomeze.

SANDRA KA HON CHU is a senior policy analyst with the Canadian HIV/AIDS Legal Network. She has worked in the Netherlands, East Timor, Hong Kong and Canada promoting women's rights.

SAMER MUSCATI is a Canadian lawyer, freelance photographer and former journalist who has worked in the fields of human rights and development in Rwanda, Iraq and East Timor.

Please visit www.menwhokilledme.com for photographs, video, news and events related to this book.